POCKET IMAGES

Vale of the White Horse

West Hanney, January 1926. Mrs Ann Sheard was ninety-nine years old on 17 September 1925. She was born, raised and lived all her life in West Hanney and is shown here wearing the traditional Berkshire bonnet.

POCKET IMAGES

Vale of the White Horse

Nigel Hammond & Jim Brown

NONSUCH

Faringdon, c.1880. A fine early panorama of Faringdon market place. The late-seventeenth-century market hall at the western end of the L-shaped market place is Cotswold in style; to the left lie the Cornmarket and Crown Hotel with Georgian frontage. On the right of the market is Portwell and a range of shops and artisan workplaces. The selection of horse-drawn vehicles attests to an age long gone.

First published 1999
This new pocket edition 2007
Images unchanged from first edition

Nonsuch Publishing Limited
Cirencester Road, Chalford,
Stroud, Gloucestershire, GL6 8PE
www.nonsuch-publishing.com

Nonsuch Publishing in an imprint of NPI Media Group

British Library Cataloguing in Publication Data.
A catalogue record for this book is available from the British Library.

ISBN 978-1-84588-388-1

Typesetting and origination by Nonsuch Publishing Limited
Printed in Great Britain by Oaklands Book Services Limited

Contents

Introduction   7

1   Towns—Faringdon, Abingdon, Wantage   9

2   The Foundries   27

3   Townspeople   37

4   Eastern Villages   47

5   Country People   59

6   Western Villages   77

7   Trade and Business   93

8   Transport   105

Acknowledgements   128

John Rocque's map of Berkshire, 1761, showing a central part of the Vale of the White Horse.

Introduction

'The Vale is broad and shallow, and slopes from the setting sun to the dawn, so that when the sky is clear, it is steeped the livelong day in light and colour. Viewed from the hills that bound it north and south, it shimmers through a blue-grey mist.' Eleanor Hayden's description of the Vale of the White Horse, written in 1907, is both evocative and poetic. Eleanor Hayden, daughter of the then vicar of West Hendred, reflected a picture of the local countryside in the first decade of the twentieth century, most notably in her book *Islands of the Vale*, but also in *Travels round our Village*, *Turnpike Travellers* and *From a thatched cottage*. She reflected a local world that has passed by: slow, insular, varied, self-sufficient and often hard. In many respects, a selection of these archive photographs helps to recreate and reflect a local pattern of life for those of us who were born and grew up in the Vale which our grandparents and great-grandparents knew. It is perhaps significant that both the authors of this book grew up in the local farming community within five miles of one another in the 1940s and 1950s, and know the Vale by the hedgerow, the enclosure road, the footpath and the field name. We both know the Vale with intimacy and hope to interpret it to a wider public, just as Eleanor Hayden did some ninety years before.

In physical terms, the Vale of the White Horse is a distinct geographical unit, being largely the catchment area of the River Ock and associated streams such as the Strutfield, Childrey, Letcombe and Ginge brooks, all bar one flowing into the Thames at Abingdon. It is bounded on the south by the grand chalk eminence of the Berkshire Downs upon which at Uffington is carved the prehistoric white horse from which the Vale takes its name. On the north is the corallian limestone ridge running from Coleshill through Faringdon, Longworth, Cumnor, thence to Oxford. This low-lying vale of Gault and Kimmeridge clay had three market towns of economic importance within living memory: Faringdon, Wantage, Abingdon. In earlier times, further market centres existed at Shrivenham, Uffington, Stanford-in-the-Vale and East Hendred. Of these, Abingdon, at the eastern end of the Vale where the Ock enters the Thames, was the most important, for Abingdon until the 1860s was the county town of Berkshire and focus of the region. Indeed the whole of the Vale lay in Berkshire until it was transferred to Oxfordshire in the mid-1970s.

The Vale is criss-crossed by routeways, pre-eminently the ancient Ridgeway and Icknield Way above and below the chalk escarpment, as well as by countless other drove roads leading across the Vale from Wales to London's Smithfield market and from the villages to market centres.

The great transport revolution of the eighteenth century came to the Vale by way of the turnpike trusts, leading to main coach-road improvement. The Besselsleigh Turnpike Trust improved the road from Hungerford through Wantage towards Oxford (1770). Other turnpike trusts improved roads in exchange for tolls between Dorchester and Abingdon (1733),

Abingdon and Kingston Bagpuize (1755), Oxford and Faringdon (1733 and 1768), and Faringdon to Lechlade (1726). Road improvement between Highworth and Shrivenham came in 1757–58; the Faringdon to Wantage and Wallingford Turnpike came in 1752.

There were also local branch turnpikes such as Buckland to Bampton (1777), Kingston Bagpuize to Newbridge and Witney (1739), Faringdon to Burford (1771), Wantage to Lambourn, and the major route south from Oxford through Abingdon to East Ilsley and Newbury (1776), broadly following the line of today's A34 road to Southampton.

The sole contribution of the canal-building era came with the Wilts & Berks Canal, which ran from Semington across the Vale of Wiltshire to Swindon, thence over the Vale of the White Horse to terminate at Abingdon (1810). This coal canal linked with arms to Wantage and Longcot (with a packhorse track up the hill to Faringdon) and wharves at Shrivenham, Uffington, Challow, Grove and Drayton. It brought cheaper coal from Somerset by way of the Somerset Coal Canal, Kennet & Avon and Wilts & Berks to the towns and villages of the Vale, but also linked to the Thames & Severn Canal by way of the North Wilts Canal, from Lechlade to Swindon, for the shipment of Forest of Dean coal. At Abingdon, the Thames linked the Wilts & Berks to the Oxford canal at the Hythe Bridge wharves in that city. The Wilts & Berks Canal encouraged the development of iron foundries and engineering works at East Challow and Wantage and also the barge building and repair enterprise at the canal's Abingdon terminus.

In the mid-nineteenth century I.K. Brunel's Great Western Railway from Paddington to Bristol crossed the Vale (1840). The local market towns were late in linking with this iron transport revolution. Didcot linked with Oxford in 1844, Abingdon with Radley (1856), Faringdon with Uffington (1864) and Wantage with Wantage road station (1875), by the first steam tramway in England. Didcot linked with Newbury through Upton, Blewbury, Churn and Compton in 1882, largely as a result of Lord Wantage's encouragement.

It is fair to say that the eighteenth century gave us the steam engine and the nineteenth century put it on wheels. This part of the Industrial Revolution was epitomized in the Vale, not just by the GWR and Wantage tramway, but also by the traction engines built at Wantage, and agricultural equipment made there and at East Challow.

In a book of archive photographs one must pay tribute to those who interpreted and encapsulated the late nineteenth and early twentieth-century scene throughout the Vale and preserved it for later generations to view.

Apart from the arch-photographer, Henry Taunt of Oxford, Abingdon photographers in this period (some of whose work is represented here), include H. J. Brooks, Warland Andrew, W.J. Vasey and J.G. Brewerton. Tom Reveley photographed around Wantage. My late uncle, Alfred Booker, photographed Grove from pre-1914 until the post-1945 period. Frederick H. Ault was a well-known Stanford-in-the-Vale photographer. At Faringdon, the studio of E. Norton Howarth saw good business and a number of his images are extant. From outside of the district, William Hooper of Cromwell Street, Swindon, and J.W. Gardner of Fairford, photographed the western limits of the Vale.

All this begs the important question as to how the present scene in the locality is being recorded for future generations to view. In these days of television, computer and the internet, one fears that high-quality photography may now be a neglected art form.

Nigel Hammond
West Hanney, 1999

One

Towns—Faringdon, Abingdon, Wantage

Faringdon, 4 May 1904. A Henry Taunt view of the sheep market. At this time, Faringdon had a market every Tuesday for corn and the first Tuesday of every month for cattle, sheep and pigs. The corn market was held undercover in the Corn Exchange of 1863 at the corner of Gloucester Street and Marlborough Street.

Faringdon, *c*.1916. Junction of London Street and Market Place. The lower portion of the market hall was used to house the fire engine and ambulance while the bell in the roof turret was used to call the crews. Anns' Garage (see p. 122) was rebuilt in 1912, but the only transport visible here is still horse-drawn.

Faringdon, *c*.1900. Three shops behind the market hall. On the left is J. Newman, registered 'shoeing-smith': these premises have now been rebuilt and are occupied by Dillons newsagents. Taylor's shop advertises wedding bouquets, wreaths and crosses, while above the doorway on the right are advertised 'harnesses of every description, portmanteaus, dress baskets, Gladstone bags and stable requisites'. A delivery boy's bicycle is propped against the door pillar.

Above: Faringdon, *c.*1960. The market hall at the western end of the L-shaped market place. The building dates from the late-sevententh century, is set on Tuscan columns and has Cotswold tiles on the hipped roof. The Georgian frontage of the Crown Hotel is to the right. This ancient coaching inn has a splendid courtyard, encompassing an early-fourteenth-century portion, and an open Jacobean staircase which gives access to a first-floor room with a distinctive decorated plaster ceiling.

Below: Faringdon, *c.*1910. Christopher Square, now an extension of Bromsgrove. The alehouse on the right is the Swan Inn. The left-hand part of the Baptist chapel has been largely demolished but the rest of the building is intact.

Faringdon, c.1920. The Corn Exchange, built in 1863, situated at the fork of Marlborough
Street (to the left) and Gloucester Street. Before the Regal Cinema (now demolished) was built
in Gloucester Street, a cinema operated in the Corn Exchange under the auspices of Oram
Bailey. He was described as being a 'smart man', invariably wearing plus fours with loudly-
coloured socks. Admission prices were 1d for one film and 2d for two performances. It was
6d per performance to sit in the auctioneer's gallery, which was colloquially known as 'cuddly
corner'.

Coxwell Street looking west, Faringdon, c.1910. The Methodist chapel on the right has been
much added-to in recent years. The cottages on the left have been demolished to make way for a
traffic roundabout.

Faringdon, *c*.1900. A Taunt view along Marlborough Street looking towards the Cornmarket. The gate on the right leads to the nineteenth-century Congregational chapel.

Faringdon, 1911. Bromsgrove with flags flying for the coronation of George V. The child on the left in the centre of the street is Dick James. Standing on the pavement, third from the right is Harry Whipp, with Mrs Harris and her son a little further down the street.

Abingdon, *c.*1890. The Queens's Hotel, built in 1864. The hotel faced the County Hall across the cobbled market and was under the management of Morland & Co; it may have been designed by Edwin Dolby, the town's Victorian architect. The hotel was demolished (together with the Corn Exchange) in the 1960s to make way for the shopping precinct, which runs along the line of the former Bury Street to the left of the hotel.

Abingdon, 1890. The County Hall situated at the eastern end of the High Street faces the market place. Abingdon was the county town of Berkshire until the mid-1860s when Reading took over the function. This fine building was completed in 1682 and cost £2,840. The general plan and elevation may be by Christopher Kempster of Burford, who was Wren's most trusted builder. The County Hall comprised a courtroom and assembly room upstairs with a covered area beneath for market trading.

Abingdon, 1890. The Lion Hotel, an ancient and extensive former coaching-inn in High Street. Today it is a shadow of its former self and much of the building was demolished in the late 1920s to make way for a Woolworths and a Prudential Insurance office. The coach entrance to the stable courtyard has entirely disappeared and the small remaining portion of the Lion is now a bakery and tea-room.

Abingdon, 1890. The Corn Exchange, built to the design of Charles Bell in 1886. Proposals were made in 1849 to place windows in the lower portion of the County Hall and to use this glazed-in area as a corn exchange. Fortunately the scheme was dropped and the Corn Exchange was eventually built on the opposite side of the market place. A statue of Ceres, the goddess of corn and harvests and the daughter of Saturn and Vesta, was erected on the apex of the new building. Unfortunately she fell soon after when struck by lightning. The statue of Queen Victoria, to the right, was presented by Abingdon grocer and former mayor, Edwin Trendell, in 1887 on the occasion of the Golden Jubilee. It was unveiled in June of that year by Lord Wantage.

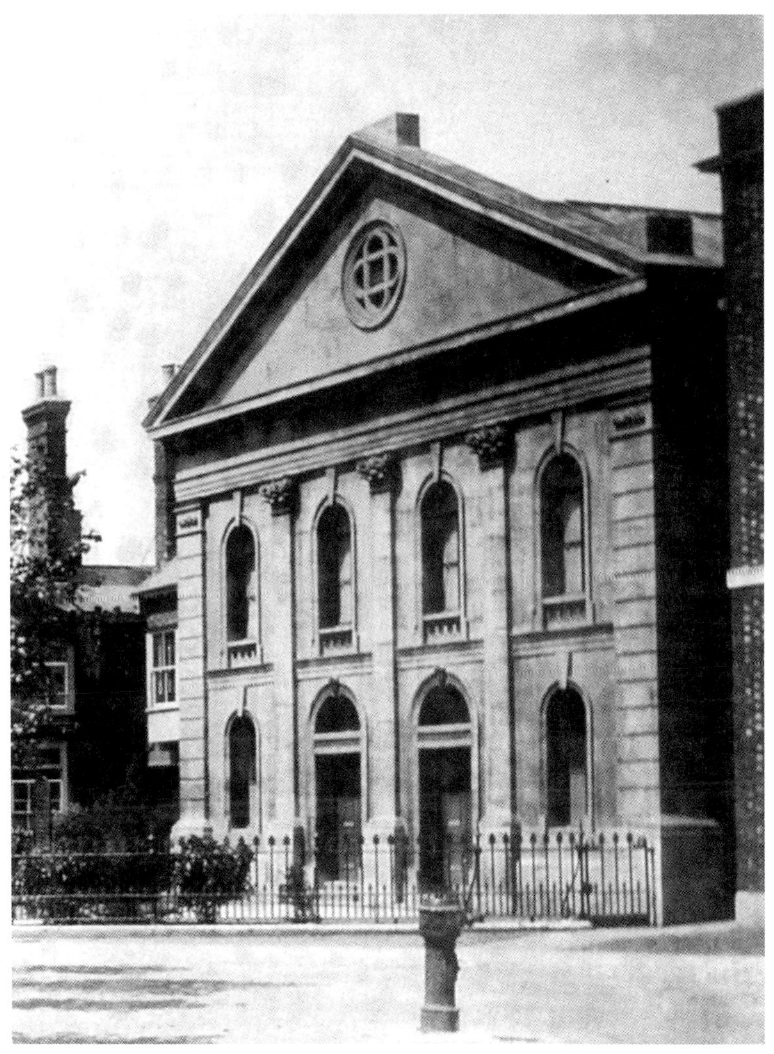

Abingdon, 1890. The Congregational chapel designed by J.S. Dodd was built in 1862.
A drinking-fountain is at the centre of the Square where the War Memorial now stands.
Following a recent period of considerable decay, the chapel and garden have been restored
to their former glory. J.S. Dodd was also the architect of Newbury's Corn Exchange which
was built in 1861–62. Both buildings are strikingly similar, although the Newbury building is
grander in both size and detail.

Abingdon, c.1890. Bridge Street on a late afternoon in summer. The Crown & Thistle is at the top of the street; the premises of Staniland's cabinet-making and paper-hanging business has a chair on the pavement advertising his trade. The Broad Face Inn, a Morland house, is at the corner of Thames Street.

Abingdon, 1890. The townscape from the Square along the northern side of Ock Street. The road was, at this time, the main route from the town to the south. Much of what stood beyond the fifth building has been demolished to make way for Stratton Way.

Left: Abingdon, *c.*1960. East St Helen Street, once known as Fore Street. This view shows one of Abingdon's architectural gems. County Hall at one end neatly complements the civic church of St Helen at the other. Beyond the church, the street led to the site of Borough Ford through the Thames, giving access over Andersey Island for a trade route towards London.

Below: Abingdon, *c.*1950. The county gaol of 1811. It was designed by Daniel Harris of Oxford and is said to have housed prisoners from the Napoleonic war. The hexagonal centre with radiating wings was the typical prison design of the period. The gaol later became a grain store and was subsequently converted to a leisure centre.

Abingdon, 1951. Roysse's Court, Bridge Street, and its garden (laid out here to celebrate the Festival of Britain). The buildings comprise the tower of St Nicholas' church, the entrance gate to Roysse's school, the magistrate's court with the former Abingdon Borough Council chamber above, and the schoolroom for John Roysse's Free School of the Holy Trinity. The school was operational on this site from 1563 until 1870 as the town's grammar school.

Wantage, c.1909. The market in 'full swing'. It was held every Wednesday for corn, cattle, horses, sheep and pigs; there was a larger special sale for fat and store cattle in April, May, September and October, a wool sale in July, and a sale of dairy and fat stock at Christmas.

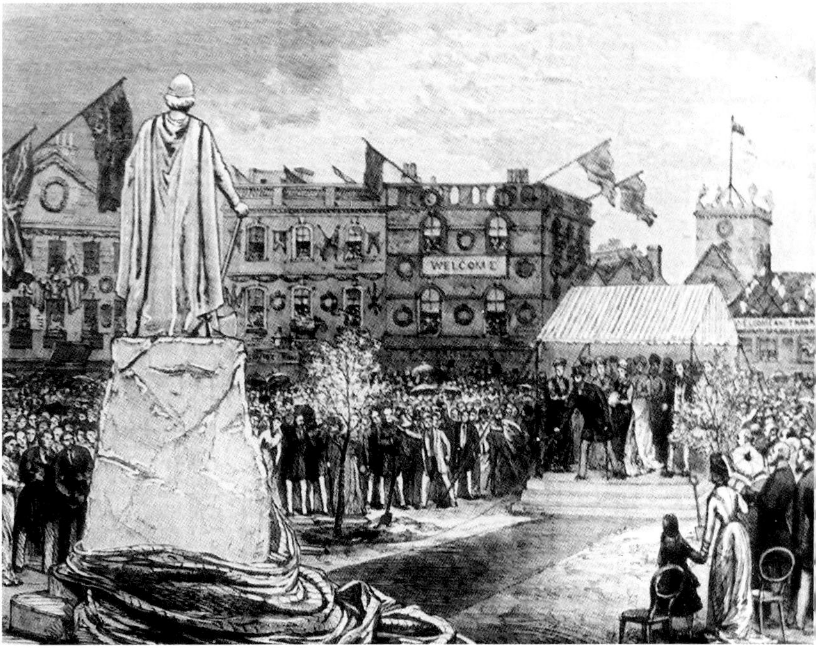

WELCOME

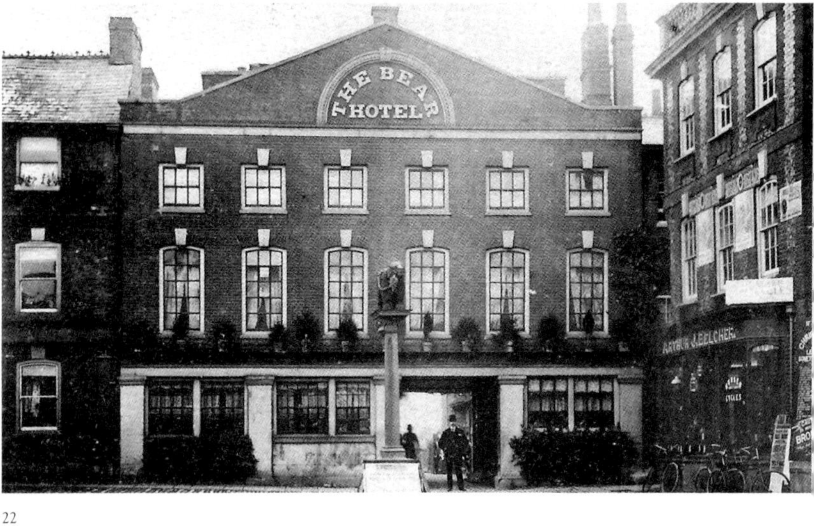

THE BEAR
HOTEL
ARTHUR J.BELCHER

Wantage, c.1930. The western end of the market place. Lewis Penney's shops are on the left and the parish church is tucked behind Kent & Son's shop in the centre. Adkin, Belcher & Bowen's office on the right now comprises the office of Green & Co. This early morning photograph shows one of the town constables talking to a road sweeper outside Lewis Penney's shop. The photographer of this image was positioned on the site of the old market hall, a substantial brick building which was demolished to be replaced by the Town Hall (presented to Wantage by Lord Wantage), which is now the Midland Bank. In front of Kent's shop also stood one of Wantage's public water pumps.

Opposite above: Wantage, 14 July 1877. This picture from the *Illustrated London News* of 21 July shows the Prince and Princess of Wales (to become King Edward VII and Queen Alexandra) unveiling a statue of King Alfred. The statue was paid for largely by Col. Robert Loyd-Lindsay, VC (later Lord Wantage) and sculpted by Count Gleichen. Nobody knew what King Alfred looked like so the face is that of Lord Wantage, presumably on the basis of 'he who pays the piper calls the tune'.

Opposite below: The Bear Hotel, Wantage, c.1906. This Georgian-fronted former coaching-inn, set back at the Western end of the market place, was on an important road-route from London to Faringdon and parts of the west of England. The cycle shop on the right belonged to Arthur Belcher; it subsequently became Penney's the ladies outfitter and is now Barclays Bank.

Wantage, *c.*1930. North side of the market place. The Cosy Tea Room is within an older building, believed to have been reconstructed to designs by G.E. Street who began his distinguished career from offices in Wallingford Street. Carved figures of Lord Wantage and Lady Harriet Wantage are on the timber of the jettied first-floor of the building.

Wantage, *c.* 1890. Henry Taunt's view of the market place from the church tower. It is interesting to see how compact and undeveloped this small market town used to be, having a population at the time of around 3,500 people. Within a few hundred yards of the market, beyond a fringe of elm trees, was open countryside. It is intriguing to speculate why the market place is so empty. By the extent of the shadows, it is early afternoon, but there are no vehicles and hardly a person to be seen on this fine summer afternoon. Perhaps this is the end of the lunch break when the shops would close, or maybe a Thursday afternoon when the early-closing day would be rigidly applied.

Opposte below: Wantage, *c.* 1930. Newbury Street, looking north towards the town centre. The building of St Mary's school was established in 1874 as a girls' boarding school and part of the teaching wing of the Wantage Order of St Mary the Virgin. The turret and spire is at the western end of the school chapel, built in 1898–99 to the design of C.E. Ponting.

Wantage, *c.*1930. Newbury Street. The Blue Boar Hotel is on the left and the Post Office Vaults can be seen in the centre. On the right, the lane leads down to Wallingford Street. The post office (now closed) and the premises of Clegg & Son (dispensing and family chemists, also at this time selling paints, varnishes and oils) are both on the right.

Wantage, *c.*1930. The market place looking west towards Mill Street and Grove Street. The Bell Inn stands at the centre of the picture, and the premises of Tom Reveley, the Wantage photographer, are on the right, wedged between the shops with striped awnings and Lloyd's Bank.

Two

The Foundries

Wantage, c.1895. The entire workforce of eighty-five men employed by the Wantage Engineering Company, photographed in the foundry yard. One of Lord Wantage's greatest services to the town occurred when he bought and extended the ailing ironworks at the foot of Chain Hill; it had faced financial disaster and his purchase saved numerous jobs and secured one of the mainstays of the Wantage economy.

<table>
<tr><td>

Specialities:

———

TRACTION ENGINES
AND WAGONS.

———

PORTABLE AND
FIXED
STEAM ENGINES
AND BOILERS.

———

STEAM MOTOR
LORRIES.

———

AGRICULTURAL
IMPLEMENT
MAKERS.

———

LIGHT RAILWAY
PLANT.

———

COLLIERY PLANT
AND MINING
MACHINERY.

———

SCREENING
MACHINERY.

———

WINDING AND
HAULING ENGINES.

———

ELECTIRC
HAULAGE.

———

CONSTRUCTIONAL
IRONWORK.

———

FORGINGS,
IRON AND BRASS
CASTINGS.

</td><td>

Above and left: Wantage, 1910. Letterhead of Wantage Engineering Company. William Hart's works of 1845 became Gibbons and Robinson, and then the Wantage Engineering Company at the beginning of the twentieth century, when Lord and Lady Wantage took a financial interest in the business, making various machinery and equipment (see left). H.G. Thurston took ownership of the concern in 1928. Challow works was formerly a stagecoach hotel standing on the Faringdon to Wantage turnpike and beside the Wilts & Berks canal. The Nalder family took control of this foundry in the mid-nineteenth century and made portable engines and threshing machines. Timber came from Bristol by canal and rail, while finished winnowing machines and ploughshares were taken to Challow Station in wagons hauled by traction engines. Cocoa-bean cleaners were made from plans taken from Germany after the 1914–18 war, together with graders, cleaners and separators for coffee plantations. During the inter-war years, the works manufactured rice hullers and machinery for brewing, malting and chocolate manufacture.

</td></tr>
</table>

Above: Wantage, *c.*1905. Wantage Engineering Company's directors with managers and foremen. Second from the left in the back row is William Booker (see pages 36, 70 and 96) but the remainder are unknown faces. It is likely that this group is assembled at the south front of the domestic building immediately to the east of the foundry buildings (all part of the manufacturing premises).

Right: Wantage, 1905. Wantage Engineering Company's notice of a devastating fire which occurred on 22 December 1905. At this time the firm specialized in the manufacture of steam engines (traction, portable and fixed), simple and compound steam thrashing machinery, traction engine waggons, steam-powered chaff cutters and boilers of all kinds. They also serviced light railways, and made colliery plant and mining machinery, electric light and power installations.

FIRE!   FIRE!!   FIRE!!!

We regret to inform you that a serious fire broke out in these works on Friday Evening, Dec. 22nd, 1905, about 10.30 p.m, which completely destroyed the whole of the Carpenters' shop, Pattern shop, Iron stores, Paint stores, Motor Assembling shop, and adjacent buildings, as well as the contents and work in progress, doing damage to the extent of about £6,000, about two-thirds of which amount is covered by Insurance.

Arrangements have been made, however, to continue our business in the meantime in the other large shops still left, so that orders will receive every attention.

Soliciting a continuation of your patronage,

We remain, yours faithfully,

THE WANTAGE ENGINEERING CO.

W. BARDILL, *Manager.*

Wantage, 1918. Wantage Engineering Company munition workers. Madame Van den Driesch, whose superior background and bilingual ability placed her in charge of a group of Belgian refugees (positioned centrally in the photograph), who found their way to work at the foundry during the 1914–18 war. Alfred Booker, who spent his working life at the foundry, recalled the story of Madame Van den Driesch approaching the storekeeper with a long list of requisitions. Arriving at the end of her shopping list, she asked for toilet rolls. Politely, the storekeeper explained that due to war rationing he could not meet her needs. With aristocratic restraint, the good lady glanced back at the next item on her list. 'Well', she enquired, 'could you possibly spare me six sheets of number three emery cloth?'

Opposite above and below: Wantage c.1875. An advertisement (above) for threshing by machinery. The primitive traction engine gives power to the threshing drum; both machines are of the kind which were developed and manufactured by Wantage Engineering Company. As seen in the picture below, ricks of sheaves are neatly built on staddle-stones; the man by the central rick is standing ready to kill escaping vermin. Despite mechanization, the operation, with at least nine workmen visible, is still, by today's standards, labour intensive.

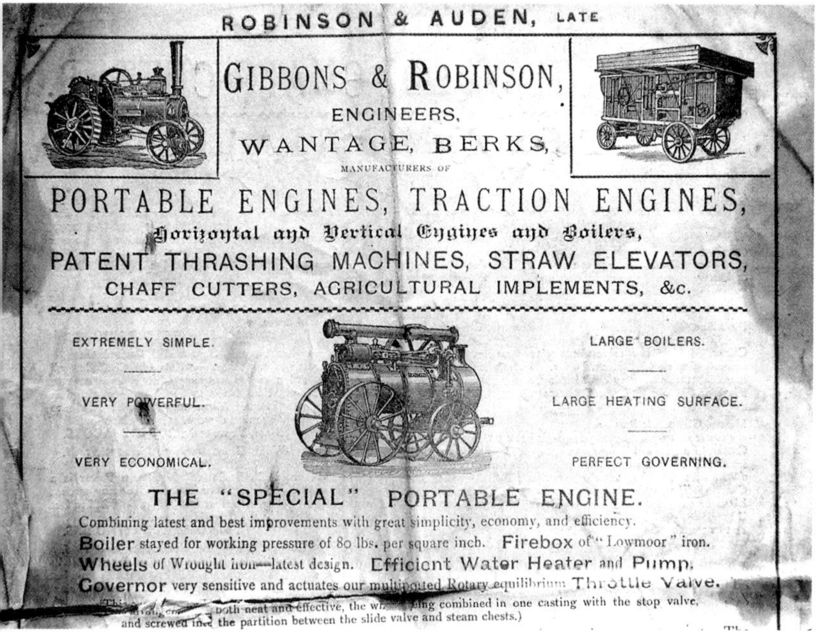
ROBINSON & AUDEN, LATE
GIBBONS & ROBINSON,
ENGINEERS,
WANTAGE, BERKS,
MANUFACTURERS OF
PORTABLE ENGINES, TRACTION ENGINES,
Horizontal and Vertical Engines and Boilers,
PATENT THRASHING MACHINES, STRAW ELEVATORS,
CHAFF CUTTERS, AGRICULTURAL IMPLEMENTS, &c.
EXTREMELY SIMPLE.
VERY POWERFUL.
VERY ECONOMICAL.
LARGE BOILERS.
LARGE HEATING SURFACE.
PERFECT GOVERNING.
THE "SPECIAL" PORTABLE ENGINE.
Combining latest and best improvements with great simplicity, economy, and efficiency.
Boiler stayed for working pressure of 80 lbs. per square inch. Firebox of "Lowmoor" iron.
Wheels of Wrought iron—latest design. Efficient Water Heater and Pump.
Governor very sensitive and actuates our multiported Rotary equilibrium Throttle Valve.
both neat and effective, the … combined in one casting with the stop valve,
and screwed … the partition between the slide valve and steam chests.)

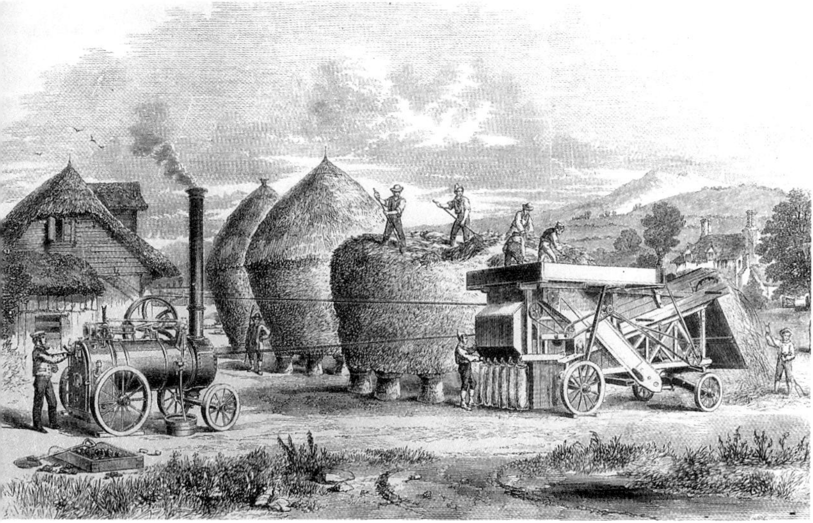

Wantage, *c.*1905. Steam-motor lorry and trailer, manufactured by Wantage Engineering Company. This was clearly a development from the traction engine and provided a more adaptable carrying mechanism for relatively light loads (see pages 120 and 127).

Wantage, *c.*1890. A Wantage traction engine in its heyday. Very similar in design to *Constance* (see opposite page) but without a nameplate or ornamental travelling-lamps, this was clearly an effective working machine.

Wantage, *c*.1900. The end of an era. *Constance* was one of the last twelve-horsepower single-cylinder steam traction engines to leave the Wantage Engineering Company foundry. Built in 1898 it generally needed two men to operate the engine: one to drive and steer and one by the tender to keep the firebox well fed with coal. Considered to be a road hazard a century ago, it is possible that a third man would have walked ahead of the engine with a red flag to warn of its approach.

Wantage, *c.* 1950. An item of heavy equipment leaving the Wantage foundry by road.

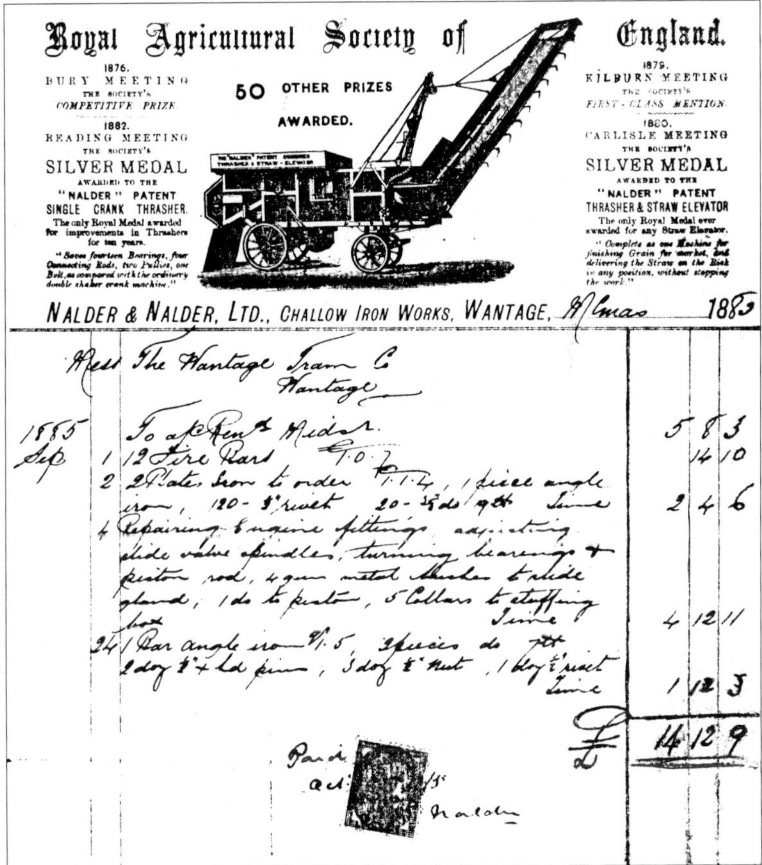

East Challow, 1885. Receipted bill for £14 12s 9d paid by Wantage Tramway Company to Messers Nalder & Nalder's Challow Iron Works for repairs to one of the tramway's engines. The billhead shows some of Nalder's specialities, namely the single-crank thrasher and Nalder's thrasher and straw elevator, as illustrated at the centre of the billhead.

Opposite below: East Challow, c.1840. Challow Iron Works, belonging to William Pierce & Co. This foundry became Nalder & Nalder's establishment from the middle of the nineteenth century, making portable engines and threshing machines as a speciality. Before becoming an engineering business and ironworks, the building was a stagecoach hotel on the turnpike towards Gloucester. This picture formed the decorative heading of Nalder & Nalder's early notepaper. Above the entrance to the works is the date 1840 with the name William Pierce & Company, agricultural engineers.

Nalder & Nalder, *c.*1890. The entire staff of the East Challow foundry photographed in the yard behind the main building. Of the eighty-seven men in this group, the apprentices are sitting in the centre of the front row, while the managers and foremen are grouped on the left.

East Challow, *c.*1923. Workmen in the fitting shop of Nalders' foundry. From left to right, front row: Michael Winterbourne, William Booker, Reginald Cross, Bert Kent, -? -, Sydney Kent. Middle row: Charles Lester, Frank Alder, Bert Jailes, Albert Kent, Sydney Rowland, -? -. Back row: Ernest Fulbrook, Tom Fleetwood, Jimmy Hammond, Eddie Fleetwood, Jack Moss, Charles Fleetwood.

Townspeople

Abingdon, *c.*1928. An early chemistry class in the general science laboratory at St Helen's school. Dating from 1903, the school was merged with St Katharine's school, Wantage, in 1938. St Katharine's was founded in 1897 by the Wantage Order of St Mary the Virgin and the nuns ran the school as part of their teaching wing (see p. 40).

Abingdon traditional morris dancers, Abingdon, c.1958. Charlie Brett, having been elected mayor of Ock Street, is standing at the centre of the morris dancers, who are shown here on the north side of Ock Street. Morris dancing has been a feature of Abingdon certainly since 1700. In that year, a black ox which was roasted in the market place caused a fight to break out between the Vineyard and Ock Street morris men. The latter group fought for and won possession of the horns and they have been paraded by the Ock Street traditional morris men each June when the whole street is invited to vote for the mayor of Ock Street.

Wantage, 1909. Funeral procession in Mill Street of Lt Napier Lindsay, son of Revd John Lindsay, who had lived at Wantage for two years. Lt Lindsay was adjutant of the 1st Royal Irish Fusiliers and was killed, aged 30, while hunting with the Aldershot Draghounds. A special train carried the coffin from Aldershot to Wantage Road station from where the Wantage tram hauled the main carriages to the lower tramyard at the foot of Mill Street.

Wantage, 1940. Wantage Town Company of the Home Guard being inspected by the Lord Lieutenant of Berkshire, A.T. Loyd of Lockinge. From left to right: Cpl A.E. Morgan, Maj. J.K. Cross, Capt. H.A. Glaysher (PTI King Alfred's School), Mr Loyd, Lt-Col. P.W.R. Carr MC (commanding 5th Berkshire Battalion Home Guard) and Lt-Col. Walton of Longworth.

Wantage, *c.* 1908. The craftsmen who had worked on the St Katharine's school extension. The workers are photographed here shortly before completion of the building; the foreman in the centre is holding out the architect's plans for the new wing.

Wantage, *c.* 1908. Building workers putting the finishing touches to the extension at St Katharine's school. The original building was erected in 1897, off Ormond Road, to the design of A.M. Mowbray as a girls' boarding school, catering largely for the daughters of local businessmen and the farming community. In 1938 the school merged with St Helen's school, Abingdon.

Faringdon, May 3, 1904. Market day, held each Tuesday (the 'great market' was held at monthly intervals). In the lower part of Church Street, farmers gather round the portable auctioneer's box for the sale of store cattle, heifers and bulls. In the market place to the right, sheep and pigs came under the hammer, while in the Corn Exchange in Gloucester Street were samples of grain, fruit, eggs, garden produce and chickens.

The town firemen on their new horse-drawn fire engine, Faringdon, 1900.

Faringdon, 1911. Roast beef in the market place to celebrate King George V's Coronation. Salutation Hotel, Portwell and Frank Cadel's shop are on the right. Townspeople of note, in a row on the left are, from left to right: Superintendent Maunders, Bob Hughes (veterinary surgeon), Dr Parker, Bert Pullen, Mr Haines (a horsebreaker and trainer). On the right of the photograph are: George Heavens, Teddy Heavens, Tommy Anns. The young boy looking over the wall behind the animal is thought to be Charles Lovesey of Fernham.

Boys' National school, Faringdon, 1921. From left to right, back row: Mr Rutter (schoolmaster), F. Whipp, W. Rouse, S. Pollard, L. Nelson, C. Stone, L. Drawbridge, G. Webb, F. Hill. Middle row: B. Brighton, R. Packer, P. Webb, F. Willis, F. Mortimer, B. Indge, F. Moore, C. Gardiner, H. Apps. Front row: C. Harris, B. Pauling, A. Giles, E. Timms, W. Tanner, G. Hiscock, R. Stevens.

Faringdon, c.1930. The Cottage Hospital fund-raising carnival. Two floats can be seen here taking part in the procession in London Street outside the Folly Inn. In the pony trap are the butcher, baker and candlestick maker, followed by doctor and nurse pushing a pram advertising Neave's infant foods.

Faringdon, 1908. A Sunday school treat—a picnic in the grounds of Faringdon House. Boys and girls, many wearing broad-brimmed sunhats, can be seen sitting on the grass. Wicker washing-baskets loaded with bread and cakes await consumption, while the proud mothers are standing on the left behind the children. The suited man with a flowing white beard is Mr Dundass, a major benefactor of Faringdon. He lived at the Elms in Gloucester Street, gave land and started the public subscription for Faringdon Cottage Hospital.

Above: Whit Monday sports, Faringdon, 1927. Mr Peter Liddiard and Miss Mary Knapp (his future sister-in-law, later Mrs Chamberlain) winning the riding/novelty wheelbarrow race.

Left: From left to right: Frank Brown of Coleshill, Charles Ashman (the foreman) of Uffington, Fred Whipp of Faringdon, Fred Page of Coleshill.

Right: Faringdon, *c.*1942. One of the painters (opposite) found alternative employment. Fred Whipp became one of the town's policemen.

Below: Wantage and Faringdon farmers, *c.* 1950. Members of the Wantage and Faringdon Farming Clubs' quiz teams at Reading. From left to right: *?* Castle, ? Knight, ? Greenslade, ? Walford, ? Smith, ? Haig, ? Buckland, Sir Roger Chance, Sir James Scott-Watson, Ralph Wightman, -?-, Archie Saunders,-?-, Ron Liddiard, -?-, Miss Allen-Stevens, Jim Manners, George Twine, Ray Gilling, Derek Pearce.

Left: Faringdon, 1945. Some boys and girls of Church Farm House school in the courtyard of Romney House, Gloucester Street. Tweed-suited Miss Alice M. Downes, the headmistress, heads the adults on the right of the steps next to the white-coated matron with her spaniel. The uniform of bright red caps and blazers was a common sight in the town as crocodiles of pupils walked between Romney House and Church Farm House in the upper part of Church Street. Among the boys in the photograph are John and Norman Carter (who later ran the grocery and butcher's shop), Nigel Hammond (author), and Frank Brooks (son of the Fernham baker).

Below: Faringdon, c.1950. Two workmen at the town gasworks: Ernie Walker and Harry Hancock with a visitor from Swindon (right). Located in Canada Lane on the west of the town, the gasworks seemed to have an unlikely position well away from the railway yard. At Faringdon, the prevailing wind would have blown the smell of the works over the town centre.

Eastern Villages

Marcham, c.1955. One of the several pigeon houses the village has possessed over the centuries. Originally, the purpose of the pigeon house was to supply the monks of Abingdon Abbey with fresh birds and eggs. In recent years, this dovecote has been splendidly restored, but the adjacent limestone barn was demolished.

Garford, c.1900. Frederick Ayris in the garden of his cottage. He was the father of Frederick Ayris (Jr) who was in business here as a blacksmith from 1925. Before then, father and son worked the forge at Hinton Waldrist. Maud Ody recalled her childhood in such a Garford cottage: 'smoky fires, well water, no sanitation, a W.C. at the bottom of the garden, copper in the shed in which to boil the clothes, Mondays washing day'.

Lyford, c.1905. A fine set of almeshouses, founded in 1516 by Oliver Ayshcombe. His memorial brass is in the chancel of West Hanney church, of which Lyford was once a chapelry.

Lyford, c.1908. A probable 'washday Monday'. This view looks toward the village school, beyond which is the Elizabethan manor house.

The village green, Grove, 1906. The ford has been replaced by a bridge over the Letcombe Brook. Timber-framed, the old Post Office had its east wing added in 1631.

The Old Post Office, seen here in 1960, burned down in 1998. The annual sheep dip took place by the bridge with flocks being driven from as far as East Ilsley. Villagers paid £1 per flock for dipping, but one shilling per hundred for all sheep coming from other parishes to the washpool (1876).

Right: Grove, inside the church, dating from 1900 (see previous photograph). Shown here is a wooden font presented to Grove by Pusey church. A brass plaque states that 'Dr Pusey was baptised in this font, 1800'. This was of course Dr Edward Bouverie Pusey, one of the founders of the Oxford Movement along with Newman and Keble.

Below: Grove, c.1920. Main Street looking south from the village green. The entrance to the church (built in 1900) is on the extreme left; the row of cottages (right) has now been replaced with modern houses. Centre-left of the photograph are old School View (left) and Rosslyn, formerly known as Dauntsey House. Chestnut trees (beyond) were in the grounds of the substantial vicarage (demolished) with Sims' Farm opposite (demolished).

Opposite below: Grove, 1908. Main Street, showing the early English-style church (right) dating from 1900. Grove became a parish separate from Wantage in 1836 when a new church was built to replace a chapel demolished in 1733. The present modern church in turn replaced the demolished 1900 building in 1965. There can be few villages that have had three new churches built broadly on the same site within about 150 years.

The manor house courtyard, Sutton Courtenay, 1890. It can be seen here that the building is ornately supported by oak columns. Two principal rooms are the hall and banqueting hall, the latter having an open timber roof and minstrels' gallery with a carved front.

Drayton, c.1895. Part of the green, village pond and unmade street leading past the tower of St Peter's church towards Sutton Courtenay. Some of the outbuildings on the left of the road, seen here as photographed by Henry Taunt, have disappeared; nevertheless a century later the basic building pattern remains much the same.

The Priory, Steventon, 1960. This timber-framed house on the Causeway may have been part of a
Benedictine cell and includes a picturesque hall which is supposed to have been the guest hall of
the ancient Priory. The raised stone causeway leads from the Priory and took the monks to Milton.

'Ye old housen', East Hanney, c.1905. A delightful row of cruck-constructed thatched cottages
face on to this part of the village green. Children of the locality play at the maypole. At this
date, it is possible to gain an indication of the age of the young girls. Until around eighteen
years of age they would always wear their skirts up and hair down. After that age it was always a
matter of long skirts and hair up.

Left: East Hanney, 1950. Cross Tree, a gigantic elm, which stood on the village green. Eleanor Hayden commented (1909) that the tree 'could shelter five loaded wains beneath its spreading branches'. It was called Cross Tree presumably because of its position near the junction of roads over the Besselsleigh Turnpike. The maypole is just discernible immediately in front of the tree, but like all local elms this tree succumbed to Dutch Elm disease; the maypole has also gone.

The Forge, West Hanney, c.1890. The village blacksmith's house and workshop were located on the northern side of West Hanney green. These buildings were replaced between the wars by a mock-Tudor half-timbered dwelling to house Leonard and Nora Barrett. Leonard Barrett was the second son of John Parker Barrett, who founded the village building firm of J.P. Barrett & Sons.

Opposite below: West Hanney House, West Hanney, 1950. Formerly called the Old Rectory, this august building is largely hidden from village view by high walls (dating from 1776) above stone causeways. This is an old building refaced in the Georgian red and blue brick local vernacular style. It is similar in detail to Rectory Farm, West Challow, the old Rectory at Farnborough and the refronted Tudor building along the southern side of Wantage market place. The house features prominently in an article on the village, which appeared in *Country Life*, 15 January 1943.

BEGGARS
CAUTION.

The BERKSHIRE, Etc., JOINT VAGRANCY COMMITTEE
HAVE ESTABLISHED A SYSTEM FOR THE

RELIEF OF ALL DESTITUTE WAYFARERS

THE OBJECT IS TO DISCOURAGE **VAGRANCY** AND TO ASSIST THE **HONEST WAYFARER.**

FOOD and LODGING can be had at Night on Application at any Workhouse, and Provision has been made, so that NO WAYFARER need want for FOOD on his Day's Journey.

All excuse for BEGGING is therefore removed, and the Committee earnestly request the Public to discourage it by declining to give either FOOD or MONEY to BEGGARS.

All Persons are earnestly requested to report all cases of Begging to the nearest POLICE STATION.

(By order of the Committee.)

HENRY E. BANNARD, Hon. Sec.

MAIDENHEAD

Left: West Hanney, 1955. 'Beggars' Caution', issued in 1911 by the Berkshire Joint Vagrancy Committee. Black and white enamel notices such as this were once in every village in the Vale of the White Horse but have been removed as scrap or collectors' pieces. This notice was for many years attached to a barn at Aldworth's Farm in the edge of the village.

Below: West Hanney, c.1960. Aerial view north from the village green along Winter Lane to Rectory Farm. On the extreme left nearest the bottom of the photograph is the Villa along with J.P. Barrett & Sons timber and building workshops. This site is now totally built-up: the Old Forge has replaced the blacksmith's workshop (centre-bottom), Castleacre is on the right of Winter Lane (bottom-right) and all but two of the remaining dwellings in the central portion of the photograph have been demolished. This is now an area of recent housing development with Rectory Farm Close extending off Winter Lane over the site of the farmyard and barns.

Above: East Hendred, *c.*1960. East Hendred House, home of the Eyston Family. Attached to the right of the house is the chapel of St Amand—one of three private chapels in England always to have heard the Catholic Mass. The house existed as early as 1291, but with the passage of William of Orange and his troops through the village, the chapel was plundered and defaced. The men broke the lamp, took away the sanctus bell, 'supped out of the Chalice taking some of the church stuffe (sic) with them to Oxford, dressed up a mawkin in it, and set it up on top of a bonfire'. There is a distinctive Mass sign set high on the right gable end.

Right: East Hendred, *c.*1960. The church tower, peeping through the trees behind the houses. In around 1902, the village was described as being 'bowered in trees' and having many fine old houses. The tower of St Augustine's church contains a remarkable and faceless clock, the fourth oldest church clock in England and the second oldest still capable of being wound by hand. It was made by John Seymour of Wantage in 1575 and operates using sarsen stone weights; at the canonical hours (9, 12, 3, 6) it plays the hymn known as the 'Angel's Tune'.

East Hendred, c.1950. A beautiful early-Tudor style building, part of which is the village shop. It may have been home to one of the wealthy wool merchants who then organized the prosperous East Hendred trade. In the early part of the twentieth century the shop was the place where a road waggon drawn by horses loaded up sides of bacon, lard and other country produce for London, bringing back such luxuries as tea, sugar and oranges. At right angles to the rear of the building a slaughterhouse, bakehouse, bacon-curing house, stables and barn were destroyed by fire on 14 June 1969.

Kingston Bagpuize, 1909. The eastern end of the village, seen from the track which leads away from Kingston Bagpuize House and the Georgian church of St John the Baptist. The house on the left was, for a number of years, the headquarters and stables for the Old Berkshire Hunt. Prior to building the village bypass, the house on the right stood at the junction of the Oxford, Abingdon, Witney and Faringdon roads.

Five

Country People

East Hanney, 1896. Four generations of the Godfrey family ready with their scythes to cut the meadows for haymaking. From left to right are: George Godfrey (1801–1898, who married Sarah Bunce in 1827), Henry Godfrey (wheelwright and sub-postmaster at East Hanney), Charles Godfrey (1852–1908, who married Susanna Tombs), Stanley Charles Godfrey (1876–1965). The latter was one of fourteen children and married Eleanor Herman.

Drayton, *c.*1890. A group of villagers pose for the camera outside the Red Lion Inn, which was then in the charge of George Brewer. On the left, a carter leads his horse; on the right two youngsters play with their rocking horse. The coachman waits for his master to emerge from the inn to speed him home in the family Stanhope gig. Might the youngish woman holding the baby at the pub doorway perhaps be a member of the Brewer family?

Above: Drayton, *c*.1885. Mrs Deacon's private school for girls at Lime Close, situated at the corner of Church Lane and Henley's Lane. Although there were a number of boys at the Dame school, this group consists of young girls in decorative hats and smart, freshly laundered pinafores. Mrs Deacon was certainly operating her school in 1854; by the 1891 census at the age of eighty-four, she had given up acting as the school's 'Dame'.

Right: The last village blacksmith, Garford, *c*.1950. Frederick Ayris came into business at Garford forge from around 1925, having taken over the concern from Mr Johns. Previously Frederick Ayris had learned his trade as horse-shoer and blacksmith from his father (also Frederick Ayris), who had worked the forge at Hinton Waldrist, but moved to Garford in his retirement (see pages 48 and 63).

West Hanney, 1906. The Butter Cross. At the start of the twentieth century, the village green was completely bare; the ancient market or cheapening cross was allowed to crumble and gradually fell apart. Stone was carted away, some to the churchyard, some by villagers to build walls. A contemporary writer noted that 'one (stone) carried the churchway across a ditch', while others were in gardens and included in the stone of the West Hanney Causeway itself or rested outside Mr Wicks' house, for he was the village mason who worked near the Lamb Inn. The re-erected cross was dedicated by Dr Francis Paget, Bishop of Oxford (1901–11) in March 1908. The task of gathering the stones was carried out by Mr P. Emmott Large of Pound Croft, East Hanney, assisted by the vicar of Hanney, the Revd C.A. Pinhorne.

Right: Garford, 1937. Basil Ayris, son of the Garford blacksmith Frederick Ayris. He is seen here making friends with one of the Rowland Baker's pigs in a sty at College Farm. It was common for villagers to keep a pig at the top of a large cottage garden. It was particularly useful during the war years, when it provided countyfolk and their neighbours with unrationed meat and offal and used up any kitchen scraps that might be available.

Below: Hanney, c.1920. A holiday group of local people. From left to right are: Clive Cottrell (who became proprietor of a butcher's shop in Wantage), Mrs Edwardes, Mr H.L. Edwardes (Hanney schoolmaster and his wife), R. Elaine Hawksford, Geoffrey Hudson. Mr Edwardes built a bungalow at the northern end of Billy Boor's orchard in Winter Lane, West Hanney, for his retirement in the 1930s; it is now known as Gigha Cottage.

Above: East Hanney, 1922. The village fête in the garden of Pound Croft. The Hanney schoolmaster, H.L. Edwardes (with his wife) is at the centre of this group of villagers and schoolchildren in fancy dress.

Left: Grove, 1922. Ronald H. Booker (1912–78) wearing boots, socks and plus-fours and a somewhat ornamental hat. He proudly holds his homemade wooden scooter. In later life he was a skilled precision engineer and was a working director of the BBI engineering company in Limbrough Road, Wantage.

Opposite above: Hanney United association football team, the 1933/34 season. From left to right, back row: J.C. White (president), John Broughton (secretary), Harry Nobes, Arthur Dunsdon, Sid Hutt, Frank Cottrell, Ben Nobes, Ernie Nobes, Bertram F. Short (village schoolmaster). Front row: Ernie Beale, Arthur Booker, Tim Lamble (captain), Fred Harris, Jimmie Beale. Harry Beale was also in the team but not on the photograph. Hanney United had that year won the North Berks Cup.

Hanney United association football team; the 1946/47 season. Having again won the North Berks Cup by beating Faringdon 5-0 at Abingdon, the team was photographed later in the year. From left to right, back row: Harry Tollit (coach), Wilf Barrow, Ben Nobes, David Taylor, Bernard Nobes, Wilf Shepherd. Front row: Fred Harris, Harry Shorter, Douglas Nobes, Bob Nobes, Percy Belcher.

Left: Lockinge, 1913. Harriet, Lady Wantage, photographed by Tom Reveley of Wantage in late October, 1913. She is with two of her house guests, their Royal Highnesses the Prince of Wales and Prince Albert on the occasion of their visit to Lockinge for a shooting party. The Prince of Wales became Edward VIII until his abdication; his brother, Prince Albert, succeeded him as George VI. Lady Wantage died in 1920.

Below: Lockinge, 1919. The unveiling and dedication of the War Memorial at the southern end of the model estate village of East Lockinge. Many of the cottages were designed with the help of Harriet, Lady Wantage; she can be seen here seated in a wheelchair just to the left of the memorial.

Grove, 1897. Villagers, assembled on the green for what was a considerable occasion, most probably Queen Victoria's Diamond Jubilee. An Order in Council appointed Sunday 20 June 1897 as the date for the celebration. Clearly, there had been a service of thanksgiving in the church during the day. Here villagers are assembled, attired in Sunday best, for tea in the marquee, at the right end of which stand at least twelve bandsmen and their drum major (probably members of the Grove Drum & Fife Band).

Grove, c.1917. Main Street looking north. This early spring photograph taken by Alfred W. Booker, the village photographer, shows boys and girls hurrying home from school. The young girl on the pavement is Winnie Clark, then approximately fourteen years old; in due course, she was to marry the photographer Alfred Booker. Nowadays, the Grove Surgery and Vale Avenue are on the right and Millbrook shopping centre is in the field on the left.

Wantage, 25 June 1929. A charabanc outing to Southsea in one of Walter and George Chandler's coaches. Mrs Kate Powell of Grove sits by the door with her son John. This all-female party is attired in typical hats of the period.

Grove, 27 June 1933. An outing for the ladies of Grove both young and old, photographed standing outside their coach having arrived at the seaside. One speculates that an enterprising photographer waited for coach parties to arrive, snapped them, and had the finished prints ready to sell to the passengers upon their departure for home.

Above: Grove, *c.*1920. A group of some thirty-three boys and girls with their schoolmaster. They are all extremely well turned out, and were photographed in the school playground opposite the church.

Left: Grove, *c.*1900. James William Booker (1875–1953) and his wife Charlotte Rosa (1870–1957) photographed by Tom Reveley of Wantage. The couple lived at Yew Tree Cottage near Grove Bridge then latterly at Old School View. William Booker was a skilled engineer and worked first at Wantage Foundry before moving to Nalder & Nalder of East Challow (see pages 27, 36 and 96). Charlotte Rosa Booker was the daughter of William Gauntlett (1827–1897) who was the village blacksmith. Later in life he worked on the Great Western Railway.

Grove, *c*.1915. The four children of James William and Charlotte Rosa Booker. They were photographed by Reveley of Wantage, sitting on studio furniture completely matching that in their parents' portrait, although the children were pictured here against a painted canvas backdrop. From left to right are: Alfred William Booker (1903–80), Dorothy Margaret Booker (1906–69), Winifred Maltilda Booker (1909–65), Ronald Booker (1912–78, the baby of the family). Winifred married Wilfred Hammond of West Hanney who farmed Rectory Farm with his brother Edward (see p.56). Ronald Booker married Kathleen Powell (1911–1998) of the village (see p.96). Alfred Booker married Esther Winnie Clark (see p.68).

Grove Platoon, Home Guard, 1941. This Alfred Booker photograph shows, from left to right, back row: A. Potter, J. Levy, P. Mahoney, Bernard Simmons, S. Wright, Cecil Wager, Ken Bosley, Godfrey Dawson, Stanley White. Third row: William Wright, Aubrey Denly, Jock Farrelley, Michael Collett, R. Levy, Richard Povey, Alfred Powell, Arthur Smith, Brian Collett, Vic Knight, Jack Wright. Second row: Edgar Povey, Robert Hatherall, Percy Symonds, ? Collett, William Fidler, Frank Murfett, Harry Batts, Stanley Irving. Front row: J. Parrott, Samuel Wright, Bob Cottrell, Percy Cook.

Left: Grove, *c.*1930. Russell Harvey and Mrs Harvey, photographed in retirement in Ramsgate. Mr Harvey was headmaster of Grove National School and Mrs Harvey (along with Mrs Hammans) was an assistant mistress. The Harveys, who taught at Grove from 1901–25, lived at Palmer Cottage in the main street.

Below: Stanford-in-the-Vale, *c.*1930. Fifty-two ladies of Stanford Mothers' Union. They are pictured with eleven children on the vicarage lawn with the Revd Edwin Farmer (vicar from 1920–44).

Charney Bassett, *c.*1920. Edward Alfred Hammond (1872–1944) and his wife Alice Anne (1873–1955) outside their home at 28 New Road. They lived here with their three sons while farming part of Manor Farm and some of Goosey Wick. Mr Hammond formed the Charney herd of British Friesian dairy cattle, which at that time was one of the first such herds in the country. Previously Mr Hammond had been coachman to an English family living at 160 Boulevard Haussmann in Paris. However, when the family wished to use a car Mr Hammond declined to be their chauffeur and took his family by way of Benson and Crowmarsh to settle at Charney Bassett. In their large garage at Charney they housed a pony and tubb which Mrs Hammond would drive; in due course they acquired a smart maroon Citroen. Their two elder sons Edward Harold (1898–1980) and Wilfred Hammond (1899–1984) farmed Rectory Farm at West Hanney where they formed the Broadhurst herd of British Friesians.

Kingston Lisle, *c.*1909. This young lad found himself a job earning 6d a week in the summer months demonstrating to visitors how the Blowing Stone operated. By blowing into the stone, a penetrating wail was emitted; it was used to call King Alfred's troops together to fight the Danes. When the boy returned home after his first week with sixpence, his mother, disbelieving the provenance of the money, gave her son a sound thrashing.

Uffington, c.1890. A summer outing to White Horse Hill. This bank holiday photograph taken just inside the north-eastern rampart of Uffington Castle shows a crowd of picnickers dressed in their best clothing. Many would have arrived at the hilltop by horse bus, others might have walked from the surrounding villages, while some might have come to Uffington wharf by 'fly barge' from Swindon, Shrivenham or Wantage from where they would walk to the hill. In the years immediately prior to the Great War it was a special treat for children from villages close to the Wilts and Berks Canal to be taken to Uffington by barge for a day out at the White Horse. Large ornamental hats and long dresses were *de rigeur* for the ladies. The woman sitting in the horse-bus has her umbrella raised to keep the sun off herself. During this period, it was remarkably unfashionable for middle-class ladies to show a hint of sunburn.

Opposite below: Shrivenham, September 1909. Military manoeuvres photographed by William Hooper of Cromwell Street, Swindon. This shows Sir Evelyn Wood and the Scottish Rifles drawn up in the High Street. Army exercises such as this were common in the Vale immediately prior to the Great War. Many took place from Churn Ranges above Blewbury on the Berkshire Downs and extended to the western end of the Vale of the White Horse (see p. 85).

Above: Ashbury. *A kill at Ashdown Park,* a stylised hunting scene painted by James Seymour (1702–52). Ashdown House peeps over Upper and Middle Woods on the left; the house was for a long time the seat of the Craven family (see p.90). Weathercock Hill is on the right with scattered sarsen stones littering the valley floor. The English painter James Seymour was (along with John Wootton, 1687-1765) a pioneer of sporting art. Seymour was noted particularly for his horse portraiture, specializing in hunting and racing scenes. The original painting is in the Tate Gallery.

Shrivenham, July 1914. The Ancient Order of Buffaloes from Bourton. They are seen here preparing to march to Beckett House fête with their banner carried high, flags flying, accompanied by a village brass band.

Knighton, c.1935. A relaxation break in the harvest field. The farm workers have been loading sheaves of wheat into wagons; family and friends have come to help. The horses have been given nosebags of barley. The young man with his shotgun will hope to bag the odd hare, which had used a shock of wheat for its form.

Six

Western Villages

Longworth, 1919. An empty pony trap waits patiently for its owner to emerge from the Blue Boar Inn. Over the years, not much in this view has changed, although the inn porch, position of doors and sign board may have been replaced, and the mud road upgraded.

Above: Hinton Waldrist Manor, *c.*1950. In early days, the St Valery family owned this partly-Elizabethan manor, and it was from their family name that Hinton gained its second name. The house then passed to the Earl of Winchester and Earl of Northampton. Charles I later granted it to Sir Henry Marten (the famous judge of Star Chamber), then to his heir, another Henry. Somewhat ungraciously, the second Henry Marten signed Charles' death warrant. In 1688, the estate came to the Loder family. During that period, the Old Berks Hunt flourished for upward of a century under their mastership. Close to the manor is a field called Doghouse Patch, the site of the kennels.

Below: Buckland, *c.*1910. A Tom Reveley photograph of the eastern front of Buckland Manor. This late-sixteenth-century house was converted in the late-eighteenth century into gothic-style stables for the Throckmortons' newly-erected Buckland house. Of the original manor remains the canted bay window, together with windows to its left and right on both floors—the rest is part of the late-eighteenth-century gothic re-design.

Right: Charney Bassett, *c.*1960. The thirteenth-century solar and chapel in Charney Manor. The house was built between 1250 and 1280 as a grange of Abingdon Abbey and is now one of the oldest surviving examples of the medieval manor house-plan. The house and grounds have for many years been run by the Society of Friends as a guest house and conference centre.

Below: The pool at Charney Bridge on the river Ock, Charney Bassett, *c.*1908. In 1908 Eleanor Hayden in *Islands of the Vale* commented, 'sheep for miles around have been brought to be washed before being driven to the great sheep fair of the county' (at East Ilsley). 'The sheep-washing trade is no longer what it used to be when hundreds were dipped in the pool at sixpence a score'.

Above: Charney Bassett, 1908. 'A turn past a couple of inns ... brings us to the village green' wrote Eleanor Hayden. 'In the centre is an ancient sun-dial raised on three steps of inconvenient height. The hollows which generations of children climbing up "to see the time" have made in them and in the pillar of the dial, are still evident. The sundial was turned into a war memorial in 1920.

Below: Denchworth, 1908. The neatly kept but unmade main street called Hyde Road. The village shop and post office are on the left. On the opposite side beyond a pony trap and cart is the thatched Star Inn—it is now a private house.

Right: A wayside cross, Denchworth, *c.*1960. Local tradition has it that this cross, some five feet in height and placed at the junction of three roads, was a preaching cross. In recent years, increased traffic caused frequent damage to the cross; in 1998, it was relocated to a green near the church. The thatched building behind the cross is the former Star Inn.

Below: Timber-framed cottages at the top end of the village, Letcombe Bassett, 1898. These buildings had walls infilled with 'clunch' or chalk block and sarsen stone in a building style typical of houses close to the chalk country of Berkshire Downs, evident also at Uffington, Baulking and Ashbury. In 1948, a plan to abandon the village and re-house residents in Letcombe Regis was thwarted. Dr Thomas Sharp called the village a rural slum but the villagers opposed this example of government post-war planning, rallying to the cry 'Letcombe is too old to die', and they won the day.

Stanford-in-the-Vale, c. 1900. A photograph by Frederick H. Ault, the village photographer, who recorded the road menders filling potholes in the unmetalled street. The elderly man with the flowing white beard in the centre is Mr Spinage, evidently in charge of his two assistants with

barrow-loads of stone. A couple of village lads look on. The Primitive Methodist chapel (1888) is now a private dwelling.

Above: A dozen schoolchildren playing on the church green on a bright summer day, Stanford-in-the-Vale, *c.*1908. A man sitting in a pony trap waits perhaps for his wife to emerge from Eggleton's shop. F.H. Ault also captured some of the tree-planting on the green; this was when lime trees were planted on the church green in 1897 to commemorate Victoria's Diamond Jubilee. At the same time twelve trees, known as the twelve apostles, were planted opposite Stanford House. At Manor Green a further nine limes were planted in 1915.

Left: Shellingford, *c.*1960. St Faith's church is one of Britain's few dedications to the third-century French girl-saint. In 1625, John Packer added the south porch, battlements and spire; this spire was struck by lightning in 1852 and rebuilt. By 1960, it was declared unsafe and a metal cap added. The ugly addition spoilt the former glory of the spire, a glory which poet laureate Henry James Pye recalled in Faringdon Hill (1774):

Lo *Shellingford, and Stanford, 'midst the train*
Of hoary trees that skirt yon level plain,
The lofty tower, the pointed spire display
Conspicuous, glittering in the western ray.

Thanks to the Revd David Peck and parishioners, the spire has been restored to its former glory.

Shrivenham, *c.*1910. An image captured by William Hooper, the photographer from Cromwell Street, Swindon. Substantial military manoeuvres often took place in the Vale of the White Horse. A number of officers are seen here at rest on the stepped pavement at the corner of High Street and Faringdon Road. One dismounted officer is caught in conversation with a mounted umpire. Stationary opposite the Prince of Wales Inn are a number of horse-drawn limbers carrying artillery pieces.

Shrivenham, *c.*1910. Lunchbreak over and it's time to move on. A group of officers and NCOs take their orders, possibly from the officer seen consulting his map in the previous photograph. The thatched cottages, left, and the house opposite on the Longcot Road still stand but the single-storey barn has gone.

Above: Kingston Lisle, *c.*1950. Kingston Lisle House, comprising an eighteenth-century block and lantern with added wings of 1840. This view of the south front looks over spacious landscaped gardens ornamented with clipped yews and Italianate terraces. The south terrace commands a view over a wooded ravine, now damned and lake-filled, towards a cool avenue of beeches sheltering the Wantage road.

Left: Kingston Lisle, *c.*1950. A fine avenue of beeches, lining the Wantage to Ashbury road on the southern side of Kingston Lisle Park, seen here in its prime. Now sadly depleted by the ravages of time and by the great gale of 1987, the avenue is but a shadow of its former self.

Childrey, looking north over the green, c.1960. The building on the left operated as the Reading Room and Working Men's Club, a gift to the village by Major Dunn of the Manor in 1896. The Methodist chapel opened in 1849 but after 137 years the south front collapsed due to frost and subsidence in 1986; the building was demolished and a new chapel built on the site.

Childrey, c.1908. Maltravers Manor in West Street dates from 1450 and is one of the oldest village houses. At the far end of the building is the west wing which was built a little later (between 1500 and 1550). The house was named after the Maltravers family of Lytchett Maltravers in Dorset; they conveyed this Childrey property to their Dorset village in 1371 to endow there a chantry to be served by three chaplains and a priest.

Left: Childrey, *c.*1960. Lesters, one of Childrey's most picturesque cottages, once comprised several dwellings and the bay window section used to be a shop. One of the village blacksmith's premises was located at the rear, with the brick building as a residual. In response to the change from horse and steam power to car, truck and internal combustion, the business placed a petrol pump in front of the old forge.

Below: The village church, Longcot, *c.*1960. In the nineteenth century the Revd John Hughes was vicar here. He was the brother of Uffington's Thomas Hughes, the author of Tom Brown's Schooldays. Inside the church is a memorial to Mrs Carter, a niece of the Hughes brothers; she and her husband went down with the Titanic. Another village member of the Hughes family was Miss May Hughes, known as the Angel of Whitechapel for her social work with poor people of the East End of London. Rest Cottage, her village home, was a holiday house for ailing Whitechapel children.

High Street looking eastwards, Ashbury, 1924. A motorcycle outrider for a grocery business poses with Ernie Taylor who holds a paint brush in his hand. This was the tool of his trade: as a young man he was a painter for the Craven Estate. Later he became a policeman.

Ashbury, c.1960. The reconstructed Wayland's Smithy Long Barrow, immortalized by Sir Walter Scott in *Kenilworth*. He came to know the area through his friendship with the Hughes family of Longcot and Uffington. The legend of Wayland the Smith as told by Scott is a fair summary. It runs thus: 'you must tie your horse to that stone which has a ring in it, you must whistle three times, put your money on the flat stone, sit down for ten minutes', and not look at the horse. You will hear a hammer clink. 'Then say your prayers and you will find your money gone and the horse shod'.

Ashbury, *c.*1960. Ashdown House, (see p.75), located on the Downs above Ashbury. It is an impressive Carolean House with a strong Dutch influence, built in 1665 by the Earl of Craven for the exiled Elizabeth of Bohemia, the snow queen. Sadly this daughter of James I died before she could make Ashdown her home.

Knighton, *c.*1946. The ancient and moated Hardwell Farm, photographed prior to demolition. The house was replaced by a modern building, but the site of the moat remains.

Buscot, 1905. Buscot Estate village, photographed by J.W. Gardner of Fairford. It is situated at the junction of the Faringdon to Lechlade road with the main street. Built in the 1890s for the first Lord Faringdon, the relatively new village hall with bell tower, clock and coat of arms was designed by Sir Ernest George. He was also architect of the village well of four square pillars and a four-gabled roof situated behind the hall, together with a number of Estate houses, two of which are evident in this photograph each side of the well.

Coleshill, 1908. Coleshill House erected in the 1650s. The building was designed for Sir George Pratt by his cousin Roger Pratt, probably in consultation with Inigo Jones. The staircase, completed in 1662, was spectacular and said to be one of the most beautiful in England. The house was gutted by fire in 1952 and subsequently demolished .

Great Coxwell, c.1930. The village shop at the corner of the road was run by the Crowdy family; it was also a post office. Mr Fred Williams, the village postman, is seen here going on his rounds.

Seven

Trade and Business

The International Stores at 14 High Street, Abingdon, c.1915. All the members of staff are outside the building, including Elsie Lowe who is positioned third from the left.

Abingdon, *c.* 1930. Fred Stimpson's shop at 149 Ock Street was advertising melons at 6d each and marrows at 4d each. Locally grown tomatoes were 1d per pound, broad beans were 1½ d per pound, and between ten and twelve bananas were sold for 1s.

Drayton Brickyard, Drayton, *c.* 1920. William Norrington was the proprietor of the brickyard in the 1850s and 1860s. The enterprise was located behind the Wheatsheaf Inn and in census returns William Norrington was listed as a brickmaker, baker and farmer. Succeeded by his son B. Norrington, he gave up the brick kilns in around 1891 to the Clarke family, members of which had found employment over the years with the Norringtons. Walter Clarke was a brickmaker and farmer from 1899 until 1935. The brickworks closed in 1938 following the arrival of the London Brick Company which competitively undercut Drayton prices with products from their newly opened brickyard at Calvert near Bicester. At the same time as Drayton closed, so too did Culham and Childrey brickyards as a result of the same competitive pricing techniques.

East Challow, 1914. An advertisement for the business of Brook Alder—dealer bailiff at Warborough Farm at Letcombe Regis where Mrs Silver, an inveterate traveller, brought back various wild animals. Brook Alder became well known as a wild animal keeper and trainer acting on Mrs Silver's behalf. In the photograph (right) he is seen in the snow, kneeling as if in prayer, before a lion.

Alfred Booker's photograph of the church choir, Grove, 1922. From left to right, standing: Russell Harvey, -?-, George Rockall, ? Dawson, L.J. Lloyd, -?-, Mark Burton, ? Woods, Alfred Booker, Victor Twyford, ? Knight, Victor Knight, Stephen Robey, Arthur Lloyd, Jim Woods, Reginald Spicer. Sitting (on chairs): Geoffrey Cottrell, Ronald Booker, Ernest Eltham, Revd Stanley Howard, -?-, Leslie Cross, Stanley Breakspear. Sitting (on ground): Frederick Eltham, Bill Mayo, -?-.

Grove, 1942. This photograph, typical of Alfred Booker's work, was taken at his youngest brother's wedding outside the old school entrance. From left to right, standing: Dorothy Booker, Winifred Hammond, Alfred Booker, Ronald Booker, Kathleen T.M. Powell, Betty Orpin, Alfred Powell, James Powell. Seated: James William Booker, Charlotte Rosa Booker, Kate Powell, John Powell.

Henry J. Brooks, photographer. He was in business in Abingdon in the late 1860s and through the 1870s; cards variously describe him as a photographer, bookseller and artist. Other notable photographers associated with the Vale of the White Horse include Henry Taunt (1842-1922) of Oxford, J.G. Brewerton of Abingdon's High Street, W.J. Vasey of Broad Street and Warland Andrew, all of whom were operative commercially from the 1890s. Tom Reveley photographed the Wantage area from his studio at 48 Market Place. He was in business from the end of the nineteenth century and became a professional photographer at the age of twenty-one (see pages 66, 70, 71). In 1894, E. Norton Howarth was a portrait and landscape photographer operating from Gloucester Street, Faringdon. Frederick H. Ault was a photographer at Stanford-in-the-Vale (see pages 82, 84). Alfred Booker was equally in demand as Grove's photographer during the inter-war and immediate post-Second World War period (see opposite and pages 68, 71). From outside the Vale, William Hooper of Cromwell Street was Swindon's best-known photographer who certainly worked between 1902 and 1922 (see pages 75). There was also J.W. Gardner of Fairford who took photographs of the far western part of the Vale before and after the Great War (see p. 91).

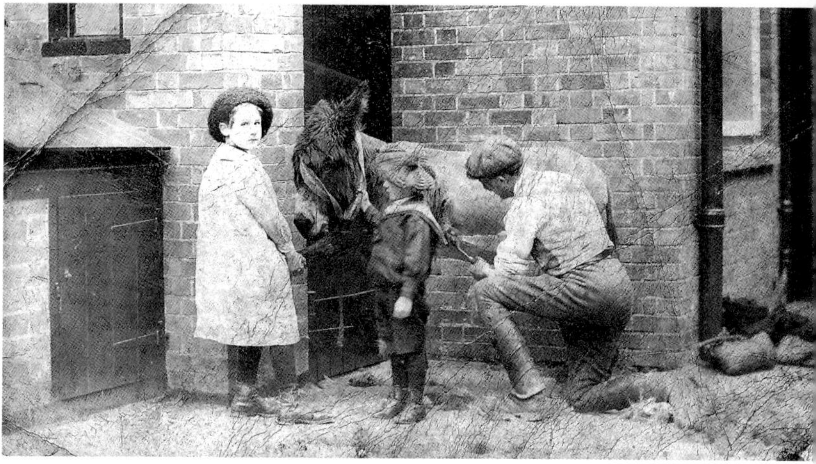

Above: Wantage, 1903. James Carvey (1855–1928) at work at his premises at 2 Lock Lane. By business he was a horse clipper and here he is seen at work with a donkey, which may well be the family animal of the two children. The elder boy is proudly holding the animal's halter while James Carvey removes the animal's winter coat.

Right: Henry N. Nichols (1848–1915), Wantage, 1914. He set up in business as a stationer and printer in premises on the south side of Wantage market place in 1875. Having arrived from Petersfield, he married Mary Ann Tosland of Newbury Street in 1876; she died in 1912. The following year Henry Nichols took into partnership his second son, John Nichols, and the business continued under the style H.N. Nichols & Son. Henry Nichols was for many years a governor of King Alfred's School and Wantage correspondent of the North Wilts Herald. He first published the annual Almanack and Directory of Wantage, Faringdon and Lambourn in 1877.

Right: A Novel Exchange advertisement, Wantage, 1916. In the days before ubiquitous public libraries, stationers and printers often ran novel exchanges or novel libraries. The Wantage Novel Library in Newbury Street retains the name of one such library, while this advertisement for Mr H.N. Nichols' business explains quite succinctly how the novel exchange operated.

Below: The Packer family and their staff at the blacksmith and wheelwright's shop, Uffington, c.1909. From left to right are: Winnie Freeman, Bill Packer, Alice ?, Ted ?, G. Day, ? Collins, Maggie ?, Bob Hollyfield, Harold Dainty, Jack Woodbridge, Bill Edwards, Aunt Lizzie Packer (with baby Queenie Packer in her arms), William Packer, Charles Packer.

TO LOVERS OF FICTION.

Your long-felt need is now a living reality

Our Novel Exchange

Is the thing you have longed for.

NOTE ITS ADVANTAGES—

We stock the best 7d. Novels, therefore — you have the "pick" of reading —

We exchange all Novels bearing our label — for the small sum of 1d. —

We save you 6d. out of every 7d. after — you have purchased the first Novel. —

We are continually adding to our stock, — including all new Novels Published. —

NICHOLS & SON,

THE NOVEL EXCHANGE,

6 MARKET PLACE, WANTAGE.

The distillery, Buscot, c. 1875. Robert Campbell established a heavily capitalized, intensive and industrialized agricultural estate at Buscot Park between 1859 and 1887. One striking enterprise was the distillery comprising the two main buildings near Buscot Lock, which operated from 1869 to 1879 and was built at a reputed cost of £100,000; it's purpose was to distil alcohol from sugar beet and make sugar. Nearby, Campbell built a mill to manufacture oilcake, a gasworks, a fertilizer works and a vitriol manufactory.

Buscot, 11 April 1935. Robert Campbell's single waterwheel-driven pump at Buscot Lock, inaugurated in 1863. It supplied water from the Thames to the large reservoir and an extensive irrigation system on the Buscot Estate. This photograph was taken by Geoffrey Dancy, a carpenter of the estate, on the wheel's last day of operation (there was also a twin-wheel pump at Eaton Hastings weir). The traction engine standing by was ready to take over pumping the water after the wheel ceased operation.

Right: Wantage, 1925. Local racing yards were serviced by businesses in the leather trade. W. Howse concluded business with local farmers as well as racehorse trainers; he also produced high quality luggage and ladies' handbags. Elsewhere in Wantage operated J.S. Trow who was a saddler and harness maker in Wallingford Street, and Cleve Belcher who worked as a leather cutter, machine-band manufacturer and boot repairer in Mill Street.

Below: Horses and their trainers on an outing, Letcombe Bassett, *c*.1960. Training establishments for race horses abound, not just in the Lambourn area but also in a number of villages near Wantage, such as Letcombe Bassett, Letcombe Regis, Fawley, East Hendred and West Ilsley.

TO GENTLEMEN USING

RACING AND . . . .

HUNTING SADDLES

GO TO

W. HOWSE,

(Son of the late D. Howse),

Saddler and Harness Maker

Wallingford Street, Wantage.

The best place in the district for new lining and fitting same

---

EVERY SATISFACTION GUARANTEED.

FIRST-CLASS PRACTICAL WORKMANSHIP

Portmanteaus and Bags carefully repaired.

STYLISH GIG AND TRAP HARNESS.

My own make.   Hand sewn.

Pony Harness from £3 10s. per set.
Cob   ,.   £4 4s.   ,, ,,.
Gig   ,,   £5 os   ,, ,,

rt Collars and Saddles new flocked from 1/8.   Warran
all new flocks.   Farm work and Stables attended to at
any reasonable distance from the town.

TRIAL ORDERS RESPECTFULLY SOLICITED.

Above: Buscot, *c.*1890. Buscot Park forestry team sawing up a felled oak, sleeves rolled up but steadfastly wearing their bowler hats. The head forester Tom Argent can be seen supervising their efforts. In common with many large estates, Buscot had an ample reserve of timber and an estate sawmill. Some of the finished timber would have been used on the estate for building purposes, gates and fencing and some sold off. Oak sawdust went to the bacon-curing houses of Faringdon and further afield: it was an excellent medium for smoking hams. Oak galls made ink and the root stump of the oak was often used by blacksmiths as an anvil base. Branches from the tree in due course might have become ladder rungs or cartwheel spokes. There was a ready market for the stripped oak-bark in Abingdon's tanneries. The finished leather returned to the area through the work of the country boot and shoe maker, the saddler and the harness maker.

Opposite below: Childrey, *c.*1950. Cress Cottage and the willow tree watercress bed, close to the spring which gives rise to Childrey Brook. The beds were laid out anew in the 1890s, using old ship timbers to create ponds in the varied-level stream, by the Rea family who owned the watercress beds. Picking the cress continued all year round except for July, when it was in flower, and January, when there was insufficient growth and was picked four bunches to a chip basket into a flat. In the 1940s each flat fetched 10s to 16s (50–80p) and was railed from Challow Station five days a week to London, Birmingham, Cardiff and as far as Newcastle-on-Tyne. Flourishing business in the early part of the twentieth century enabled the Rea family to extend the Childrey beds, purchase the Letcombe Bassett beds and rent those at Kingston Winslow and Ashbury.

Right: Abingdon, 1905. The wife of George Mobbs, Mrs Miriam Mobbs, started this boot and shoe business in 1885 under her husband's name. Originally it was located elsewhere in Bath Street in a building now occupied by Adkin & Co. George Mobbs was an agent for the Prudential Assurance Co. and Norwich Union. At the beginning of the twentieth century he would most likely have plied the boot, shoe and repairing trade whilst travelling the villages around Abingdon collecting insurance premiums. The business passed to Percy Mobbs and latterly to his son Jack Mobbs. The day-to-day running of Mobbs & Son is now in the hands of Jack Mobbs' daughter Mrs Valerie Greader. This elegant and informative advertisement indicated the range of the work undertaken, as well as some of the attractive boot and shoe prices.

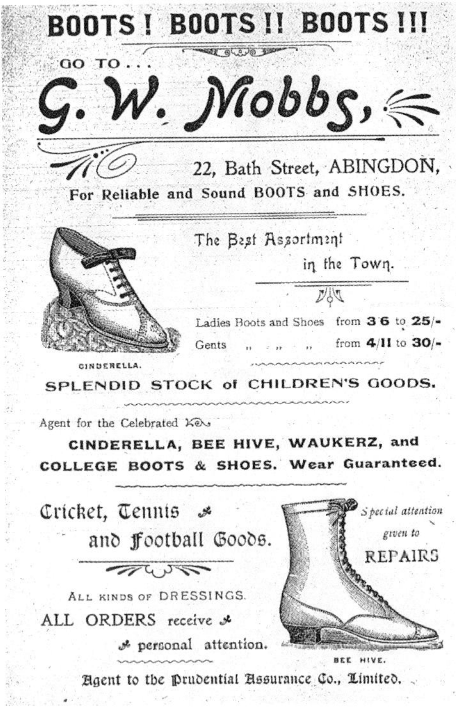

Left and below: Wantage, 1919. Advertisement for the wares of J.N. Arbery & Son at their market place shop. John Nicholas Arbery continued the business under his own name from 1894 having previously run the enterprise with Jesse Lay as Lay & Arbery. J.N. Arbery's son Howard took over in 1920. In 1951 the business became a limited company on a family basis as Arbery & Son Ltd. John Arbery, grandson of the founder, closed the business in 1997. The Victorian shopfront of London House (below) with the neat barley sugar posts at the corners of the windows, had wartime traffic damage repaired under the watchful eye of Wantage resident John Betjeman. Frosted upper windows advertised costumes, millinery, corsets, and mantles. Behind the Georgian brickwork is an L-shaped timber-framed Elizabethan building of some stature which extends to three floors.

Eight

Transport

Uffington, c.1919. The postman, standing with his bicycle on the lifting bridge over the Wilts & Berks canal at Uffington Wharf. At that time Wharf Farm was in the hands of John Jenkins who was also a haulier. He was the last man, so it is said, to operate a barge on the canal, hauling salt and coal from Swindon to Wantage. He also carried timber up and down the canal for the Craven Estate, maintaining for the purpose a team of greys as superior tug-horses. The last use of his barge was to carry hay back to Wharf Farm from canal-side meadows. Across the canal just below the bridge it is possible to make out the rotting hulk of one of Jenkins' barges.

The Wilts & Berks Canal at Caldecott Walk, Abingdon, 1890. The canal passes under Caldecott lifting bridge to enter the basin at the eastern terminus of the canal; the wharf buildings, timber yard, warehouse and boat-repairing yard are visible in the distance. The canal to Abingdon was opened in 1810, closed in around 1906 and abandoned by 1914; its function had been to bring cheap coal to the Vale of the White Horse from Somerset and the Forest of Dean. The year of 1838 saw 9,930 tons of coal being unloaded at Abingdon, 1,885 tons at Wantage, 1,668 tons at Challow, 546 tons at Uffington and 2,804 tons at Longcot (largely for Faringdon and surrounding villages). By 1870, with competition from the railway, tonnages had fallen to 340 tons at Abingdon, 93 tons at Challow and 109 tons at Longcot.

Right: Wilts & Berks Canal, 1883. An advertisement for barge services found in Astill's Swindon Almanack. It is evident from this information that the Midland, Western and Metropolitan Co. carried coal from the Forest of Dean and Radstock to the Vale, and foundry coke to Challow and Wantage for use in the engineering works.

Below: Wantage, *c*.1958. This Bath Stone wharf manager's dwelling is located next to the wharf at the foot of Mill Street, at the end of the Wantage arm of the Wilts & Berks canal.

Midland, Western, and Metropolitan
CANAL CARRYING COMPANY, LIMITED,
(WILTS AND BERKS CANAL,)
GENERAL CARRIERS
Of Merchandise and Goods of all kinds.

WHARVES AT

BRISTOL,	DAUNTSEY,	LONGCOT,
BATH,	WOOTTON BASSETT,	CHALLOW,
BRADFORD,	HAY LANE,	WANTAGE,
MELKSHAM,	WROUGHTON,	ABINGDON,
LACOCK,	SWINDON,	CRICKLADE,
CHIPPENHAM,	STRATTON,	STROUD and
CALNE,	BOURTON,	GLOUCESTER,
FOXHAM,	UFFINGTON;	

ALSO, LANDINGS AT OTHER PLACES.

FREIGHTS CARRIED IN COMPANY'S BOATS,
Which run regularly between Swindon and Bristol ; and elsewhere as required.

Through Rates Quoted for Full Loads.

IN COMMUNICATION WITH ALL PARTS.—RATES ON APPLICATION.

BRISTOL DEPOT AND WAREHOUSES,
COUNTERSLIP.

Best Forest, Somerset, and Smith's Coal, Foundry Coke and Small Coal,

GARDEN GRAVEL
And Road Materials Always in Stock.

Goods of all descriptions Carried at Moderate Rates.

For Dates of Company's Boats between the above places, carrying less than full loads, and for freights, general information and full particulars, apply to

H. G. ALLEN, Manager,
Canal Office, Swindon.

Wilts & Berks Canal at Wantage wharf during the last few years of the canal's economic activity, *c.* 1895. Major products carried were building materials and ballast, some coal, grain and flour to and from Wantage mills. Some building materials are in view here stacked in front of Wharf Terrace: kitchen sinks, chimney pots and drainpipes.

Canalside cottages at Grove wharf, Wilts & Berks canal, *c.*1957. They later became known as Ormond Row. They started as a lock-keeper's cottage, but were extended to form a row of four wharf-workers' cottages and additional stabling, all backing on to the canal.

Steventon, 1955. One of the last limestone and brick hump-backed bridges over the Wilts &
Berks Canal. This bridge carried the Steventon to East Hanney road over the waterway; it was
demolished to enable larger lorries to use the road.

Great Western Railway, c.1850. A print by J.C. Bourne of a down passenger train, broad gauge,
at Pangbourne. This view of an early broad gauge railway would be typical of such Vale stations
on the main line of 1840 to Bristol, as Steventon, Wantage Road, Challow, Uffington and
Shrivenham at the same period, just a few miles down the line, standard gauge was adopted in
the 1890s.

Wantage Road Station, c.1890. In this view looking east from the down platform, Henry Taunt photographed the early brick bridge, which took the Besselsleigh Turnpike (now the A338) over the tracks. The booking office and stationmaster's house is on the right, and standing across the middle of the photograph is the whole station staff, on parade shortly after transfer from I.K. Brunel's broad gauge to standard gauge tracks. It is believed that the horse was used to move Lord Wantage's slip coach into the station yard: he was permitted by the GWR to have a carriage detached from any through-train.

Faringdon, c.1919. Faringdon Station, opened in 1864, at the end of the branch line from Uffington. Engine sheds can be seen on the left; the passenger station is beyond the signal box with the goods and shunting yard on the right.

Right: Wantage, 1916. A price list of third-class cheap day tickets from Wantage to further afield, including both tram and rail fares. The price of 8s 7d (43p) for a return from Wantage to Paddington now seems something of a bargain.

Below: Grove, *c.*1905. Thomas William Gauntlett (born 1849) at Grove, is seen here on the footplate of this 850–class saddle tank engine No. 959. He was the eldest brother of Charlotte Rosa Booker (see p.70). This posed photograph with fireman standing proudly beside the engine was probably taken at the GWR works at Swindon. In retirement Thomas Gauntlett lived at Fairview Cottages in Grove.

WANTAGE
TRAMWAY Co., Ltd.

AGENTS TO THE G.W.R.

GENERAL HAULIERS,
FURNITURE CAREFULLY REMOVED.

Tickets at a Return Fare of 6d. each,

Will be issued to anyone wishing to go to the Station
to see off or to meet friends on the understanding
that they return by the same car.

Cheap Return Tickets,

ISSUED TO PARTIES OF 12 AND OVER 6d. EACH

Market Tickets

Will be issued each Saturday for the convenience of Passengers
from Hanney and Grove to Wantage.

Return Fares as follows :—

    From Station to Wantage and back - 6d.

      ,,   Oxford Lane ,,   ,, - - 4d.

      ,,   Grove Bridge ,,   ,,   - - 2d.

    Available to return same day only.

Trams meet all Trains stopping at Wantage Road Station.

For further information, apply to—

W. A. NOBLE, Manager

Left: Wantage, 1916. A price list of cheap offers for travel on the Wantage tramway between Wantage Road Station and Wantage Mill Street terminus and intermediate stops.

Below: Wantage Tramway, September, 1923. A well-known cartoon (below) drawn by E.C. Float. The artist, who worked at the Royal Mint in London, created the cartoon while on holiday at the Bell Inn at Grove. Arthur Hitchcock was born in 1863 and came to Grove in the 1890s from Eynsham; he was the local chimney sweep and the hero of this cartoon. In 1895 while working for GWR he lost a leg in an accident on the railway. While returning home to Kent's Row in Grove his donkey took fright and bolted when the Wantage tram was about to overtake. Despite all Arthur's efforts to halt the animal, it gathered speed and outpaced the somewhat slow tram. Thousands of these postcards were printed at the time, and have been reprinted since. Arthur Hitchcock died in 1942.

Jane, c.1960. The No.5 engine, belonging to Wantage Tramway Co., was affectionately known as *Jane*. It was a George England well-tank engine, built in 1857 and purchased by the tramway in 1878. For many years it was the workhorse of the fleet and this engine once stood on show beside the down platform at Wantage Road Station. The engine is seen here resplendently repainted; it is now kept at Didcot Railway Centre.

Left: Upper portion of the Wantage Tramway Co. office in Mill Street, Wantage, *c.*1965. The ornamental top of this 1904 building in yellow and terracotta brickwork has now been removed for safety reasons. Edwin Dolby of Abingdon was architect to the tramway company and this would have been one of his last commissions. Entry to the booking office and waiting room was at street level – this also led to the platform and trainshed.

Below: The passenger tramway yard at the town's terminus, Wantage Tramway Co., *c.*1892. The yard looked towards the town gasworks which was situated close to the goods terminus at the foot of Mill Street. It can be seen that passenger car Nos. 1, 2 and 3, were fully laden and being hauled by Hughes' tram engine. This Henry Hughes engine was made at the Falcon Works, Loughborough, in 1877 and purchased by the tramway company for £600. It was scrapped in 1920.

Above: Tramway engine No. 6 in the passenger terminus at Wantage, *c.*1911. The engine was built in 1880 at the Culford Iron Works, Ball's Pond, London, under the supervision of F.W. Jackson. It was bought for £60 in around 1882 on a trial basis, the payment not being made until 1888. The engine continued in use until 1925 but was sold for scrap to W.G. Keen & Co. of Bristol and broken up at Wantage in around 1931.

Below: Wantage tramway Co., *c.*1911. The Hughes' tram, hauling car Nos. 1 and 3, has stopped on the way to Wantage by the side of Grove Park. The stationmaster's house and the road bridge at Wantage Road Station are visible in the distance.

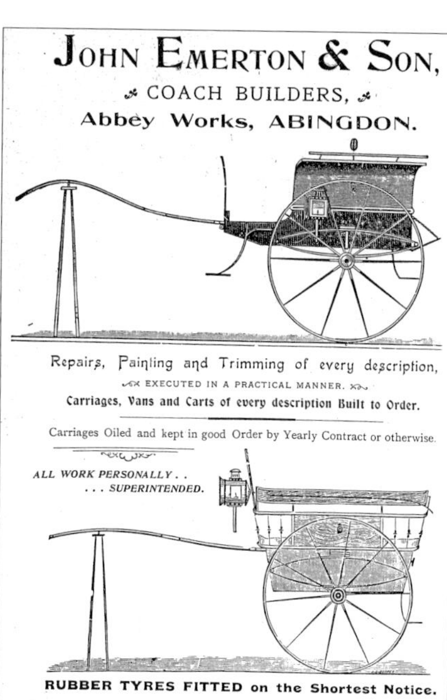

Left: Abingdon, 1905. John Emerton's coach building and repair business located at 22 The Abbey. Unfortunately for this line of business, coaches were shortly to be superseded by the motorcar and garage. This family concern, which produced Stanhope Gigs and Governess Carts as illustrated, had by 1936 become Emerton (Abingdon) Ltd. motor body, coach builders and wheelwrights at the Phoenix Iron Works, Abingdon.

Below: Marlborough Street, Faringdon, c.1895. On the right of this photograph is Arthur's Hill, a raised pavement named after H.N. Arthur's coach and harness-making business. One coach is inside the building while another awaits attention on the pavement; a pair of shafts is propped against the wall. Notice how the goods were raised and lowered from Arthur's Hill using a hoist up to the second floor workshop. This hoist could swing inside the building when not in use.

Right: An advertisement from 1903 for part of Coxeter & Andrew's wide-ranging business. Of particular interest is the household removal service, and this trade illustration of their horse-drawn removal van is characteristic.

Below: Coleshill, *c.*1908. Horse-drawn vehicles tended to fall into two types—those with two wheels and those with four. At the height of their popularity they were just as varied as cars are today. Private horse-drawn vehicles often reflected the taste and aspirations of the owner; they could look smart and expensive, vulgar, affluent or poor and hardworking, even youthful and dashing.

Abingdon, *c.*1890. A youthful cricket team (possibly), on an outing. The group was being driven off here from the gravel playground of Abingdon School in a horse-drawn Waggonette.

Eaton Hastings, *c.*1910. A virtually empty road, serving to remind us of one of the advantages of the horse-drawn era. This is the main road from Lechlade to Faringdon, part of today's busy A417. On a wet day in 1910 it must have been all but impossible to cross a road without getting one's shoes and clothing thoroughly wet and muddy.

A Wantage Engineering Co. traction engine, Wantage, 1920s. This vehicle was typical of several which would ply the Vale country roads travelling from farm to farm, hauling tackle to complete the threshing of the harvest. Thatcher & Co. had such a business located in Abingdon railway yard, close to the former Railway Inn. On a contract basis they would haul a threshing drum and elevator in autumn and spring months, staying at one farm for two or three days to clear the rickyard before moving to their next appointed farmer.

Stanford-in-the-Vale, *c.*1920. A fine example of one of Clay's steam wagons. This was a vehicle which was halfway between a modern truck with a diesel or petrol engine and a steam traction engine.

An unmade road, running up the chalk escarpment of the Berkshire Downs to the Ridgeway and on to Lambourn, Kingston Lisle, *c.*1909. Travellers on roads in the chalk country experienced different problems to those in the clay vales. As well as mud in wet periods, dry months created a fine white dust which rose in clouds behind a drove of sheep, farm waggon or private gig, and in places gave rise to such road names as White Shoot (Blewbury), White Road (East Hendred), and White Hill (Bishopstone).

Great Coxwell, 1917. A rare opportunity for villagers to inspect an aircraft at close quarters, let alone see one flying. This Royal Flying Corps army aircraft was forced to land in Black Furlong on R.S.P. Smith's Colleymore Farm. Note the Lewis machine gun mounted above the nose of the aircraft.

The Wantage Motor Company's advertisement, 1919. It was one of the first filling stations and garages in the town, located strategically at the corner of Mill Street and Grove Street on the main roads out of the market place to Oxford and Faringdon. Consequently it attracted increasing business as the internal combustion engine replaced the horse and steam-hauled transport.

Anns' Garage in Cornmarket in the very early days of motoring, Faringdon, 18 May 1912.
Harry Robins can be seen (left) with Edgar Argent. Apart from advertisements for Michelin
tyres, Pratt's motor spirit, Shell, and puncture repair by vulcanization, the shop window (left)
carried a considerable display of carbide lamps used for headlights. This is the last phograph
of the Anns building before they moved their premises across the road.

Grove, c.1933. Miss Kathleen Powell riding pillion on the local milkman's very primitive single-cylinder motorcycle. The rider is believed to be Frank Little.

Buckland, c.1920. Leonard Barrett, second son of John Parker Barrett (a builder of West Hanney). He was driving this early touring car, photographed quite possibly on the road leading into Buckland village. One of the passengers is Olive Barnes, the other could be Nora Barrett.

Ashbury, 1923. A church outing to Bournemouth in one of Mr Rimes' Swindon coaches. Mr Rimes insisted on having Swindon's coat of arms painted on the side of his coaches, which led to a protracted dispute with the Borough Council. At one stage, council workmen were sent at night to paint out the arms. The matter ended in the law courts.

One of Tommy Clare's two coaches, taking villagers on a day trip to Weston-super-Mare, Little Coxwell, c.1930. Mr Clare's coaches developed into Eagle Coaches of Faringdon. From left to right are: Mrs Austen, Mrs Seaford, -?-, -?-, Mr Angless, Mrs Angless, Charles Stratton, Billy Austen, Bill and Arthur Austen (the young twins).

Above: Shrivenham, 1912. This high, leaf-sprung pram with thin, solid rubber tyres was typical of the time. The two-year-old twins in the prams together with the two girls (who later became Mrs Lawrence and Mrs Dance) were about to be taken to Beckett House fête.

Right: Faringdon, *c.*1930. The 'sit-up-and-beg' bicycle was an ideal way to travel the towns and villages of the Vale. Miss Cadel (later to be Mrs Burgess) has decorated herself and her bicycle in oriental fashion for the Faringdon Hospital Carnival.

R. S. Langford & Sons,

Coal, Coke, . . .

and Corn Merchants.

Factors of

House & Steam Coal of every description.
Welsh Smokeless Steam and Smiths' Coal.
Gas, Foundry and Furnace Coke.
Breeze, Patent Fuel, Firewood, &c.

Delivered at Lowest Prices, in Town or Country,
. . . in large or small quantities.

Our Cash Price List for Truck Loads will compare favorably with that of any advertising Firm. Our large and increasing connection in the district enabling us to give consumers every advantage. . . . .

PRICE LISTS ON APPLICATION.

Postal Address:
G.W.R. STATION,
ABINGDON.

Telegrams:
LANGFORDS, ABINGDON.
Telephone No. 43.

MOIRA, ...
CANNOCK CHASE
BEST BLOCK, . .
and other high-class
House Coals kept in stock.

Also a large selection of lower priced qualities to suit every requirement.

Depôts:—Challow, Steventon, and Abingdon Stations.

Abingdon, 1905. Langford's, one of the two substantial coal merchants in the Vale. The other was Weedon's, but they operated mainly from Goring, Wallingford, Wheatley and Watlington. R.S. Langford & Sons operated from Challow, Steventon, Uffington, Faringdon and Abingdon, although their rail coal-wagons did not always bear all these place names. They also dealt in corn and it was known for one or other of their coal wagons to arrive at Abingdon or Wantage Road Station loaded with grain, but carefully sheeted with tarpaulin.

Wantage Engineering Co., c.1905. A steam lorry with solid wheels made at the Wantage Foundry. It is seen here in use by the town of Uitenhage which is some twenty-five miles from Port Elizabeth in South Africa. This photograph certainly attests to the considerable export market that existed for this Wantage ironworks.

The effects on the Vale of the 'great blizzard', West Hanney, 1962–63. It can be seen from this photograph that the six-foot snowdrifts were beginning to melt in Winter Lane, north of West Hanney. This enabled the GPO Morris J2 van to work at replacing fallen telephone wires.

Acknowledgements

I am grateful particularly to the following people and organizations:
Abingdon School Archives (Mr Michael St. J. Parker), Mr John Arbery (Wantage), Mr Basil Ayris (Abingdon), Mr Alan Steeves-Booker (Shorncote), Jim Brown's photographic collection (Fernham), Mr F.E.J. Burgiss (Wantage), Executors of the late Mrs K.T.M. Booker (Grove), Mrs Yvonne Drakes (Cabourne), Mrs E Fletcher (Abingdon), Drayton Local History Group, Mrs Valerie Greader (Abingdon), Committee of Hanney War Memorial Hall, Mr Fred Harris (East Hanney), Mr Jack Mobbs (Abingdon), Mr Rowland Hill (Faringdon), Oxfordshire Library Service (Abingdon Local History Collection), Mr Hugh Randolph (Abingdon), Mr & Mrs N.W. Stimpson (Drayton), St Helen's School Abingdon (Mrs Galloway), the Society of Friends (Charney Bassett Manor), the Tate Gallery, Mrs Ann Townsend (Grove), University of Cambridge Library, University of Reading, Vale & Downland Museum (Wantage), Wiltshire Library Service (Swindon Local History Collection), Mr Barry Winter (Drayton), and to many other people who have offered either purposely or inadvertently, information which has been useful in assembling this book.

Books and publications consulted:

Islands of the Vale, Eleanor Hayden (1908), *Rural Life in the Vale of the White Horse* (1974, reprinted 1993), *White Horse Country* (1972), *The Book of Abingdon* (1979), *The Oxfordshire Village Book* (1983), Nigel Hammond, *Victorian Wantage*, Kathleen Philip (1968), *A Guide to the Churches of Oxfordshire*, Jennifer Sherwood (1989), *An Artist's Walk through Old Grove*, Bill Fuller (Five books 1986-90), *The Length of the Road – Garford, Lyford, Charney Bassett*, Maud Ody (1985), *The Wantage Tramway*, S.H. Pearce-Higgins (1958), *The Wilts & Berks Canal*, L.J. Dalby (1971), *Childrey*, J.M. Drummond & Dennis Bradbrook (1989).